The
BIRDING
LIFE

The BIRDING LIFE

A PASSION *for* BIRDS *at* HOME *and* AFIELD

Text by LAURENCE SHEEHAN
Photographs by WILLIAM STITES
with CAROL SAMA SHEEHAN *and* KATHRYN GEORGE PRECOURT

CLARKSON POTTER/PUBLISHERS
New York

Published in the United States by Clarkson Potter/Publishers, an imprint of the
Crown Publishing Group, a division of Random House, Inc., New York.
www.crownpublishing.com
www.clarksonpotter.com

CLARKSON POTTER is a trademark and POTTER with colophon is a registered trademark
of Random House, Inc.

Library of Congress Cataloging-in-Publication Data is available upon request.

ISBN 978-0-307-71635-4

Printed in China

Book and jacket design by Wayne Wolf/Blue Cup Creative
Jacket photographs by William Stites

Additional photography credits: pages 14, 15, Brian E. Small; page 32 (above), Roger Tory
Peterson Institute; page 32 (below) from *A Field Guide to the Birds* by Roger Tory Peterson.
Copyright © 1934, renewed 1961 by Roger Tory Peterson. Used by permission of Houghton Mifflin
Harcourt Publishing Company. All rights reserved; page 57, Deborah Allen; page 83 (left), Bill
Thompson III; page 195, Kenn Kaufman; page 201, Todd Oldham.

10   9   8   7   6   5   4   3   2   1

First Edition

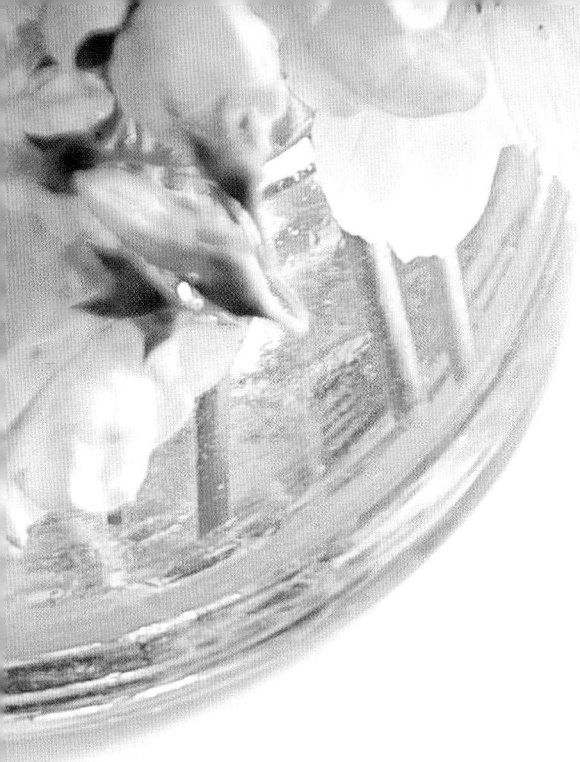

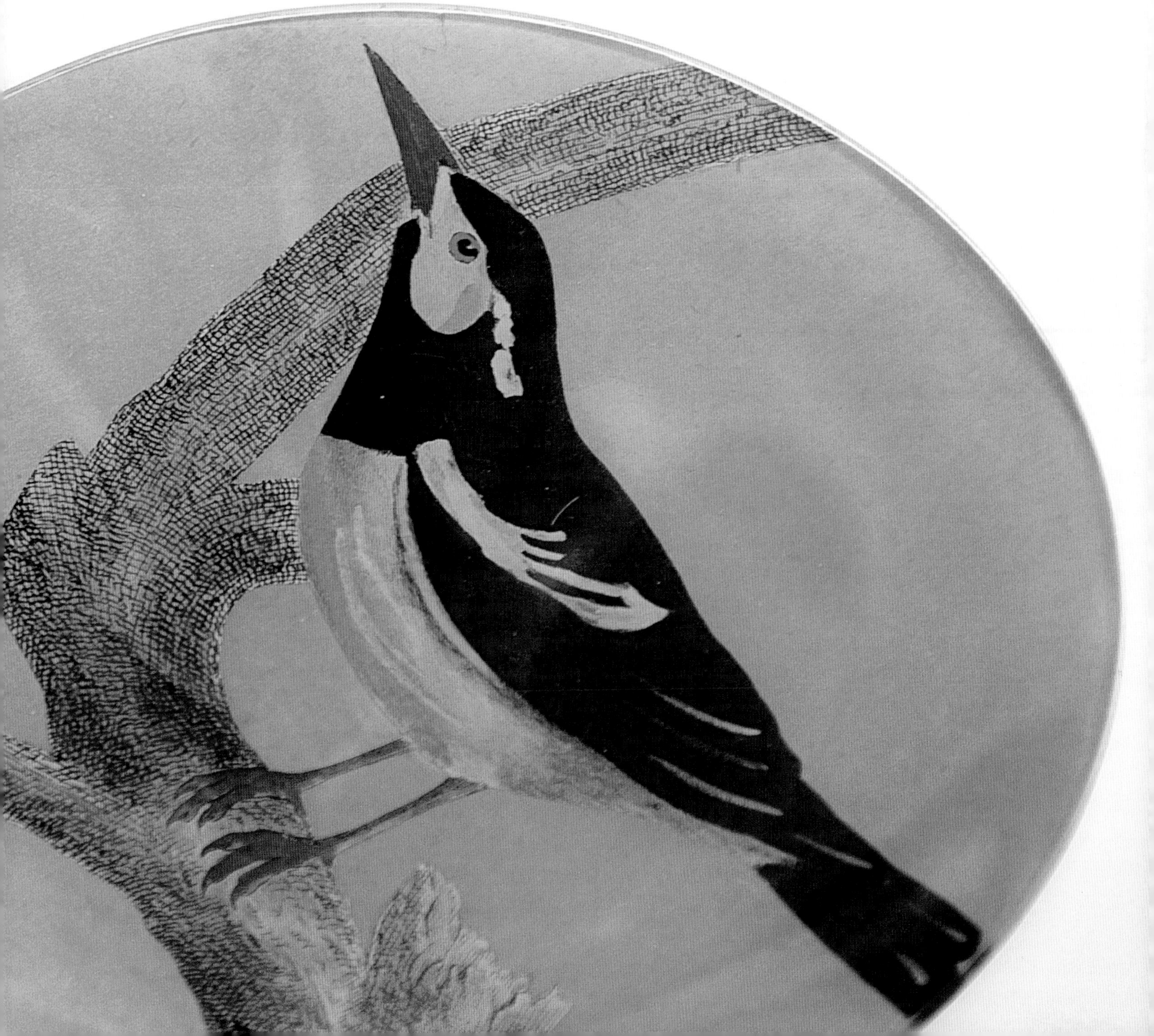

CONTENTS

PART III: AT HOME WITH BIRDS

PROLOGUE
THE QUEST FOR BAIRD'S SPARROW

UNDER THE STEELY GAZE OF A TWO-STORY-HIGH STATUE OF A SIOUX INDIAN, THE SCHOOL BUS WITH TWENTY BIRD WATCHERS ABOARD PULLED OUT OF THE CHIEFTAIN MOTEL PARKING LOT AT 5:00 A.M. ON THE DOT. IT WAS PITCH-BLACK IN CARRINGTON, NORTH DAKOTA, AT THIS UNGODLY HOUR. THE STREETS WERE VACANT. LEAVING TOWN, WE SPED ALONG A TWO-LANE HIGHWAY SURROUNDED BY VAST FIELDS OF WHEAT AND SOYBEANS.

The bus passengers were sleepy but not sullen. The early robin gets the worm, and bird lovers routinely set their alarm clocks for pre-dawn wake-ups in order to see birds during their hyperactive early morning ablutions. Some riders nodded off. Others murmured with their seat companions about the day's prospects for seeing "lifers"—birds never before seen in the flesh by an individual and, once seen, eligible for a check mark next to their names on the individual's "life list." Everyone was dressed in field clothes, weathered outfits in drab colors, not the camouflage gear of hunters, but close. All of us were armed with binoculars, and the more affluent also carried $3,000 spotting scopes capable of bringing distant birds so close you could almost ruffle their feathers. Still other birders hugged tripods mounted with mammoth long-lens cameras of the kind used by professional photographers at major sports events.

PRECEDING PAGES: Artist and naturalist Julie Zickefoose stalks a marsh-dwelling bird, the sora, in central North Dakota, while her assistant, using an iPod, lures the bird using its own song, "a plaintive whistled *ker-wee.*" OPPOSITE: Participants in the annual Potholes & Prairie Birding Festival train their cameras, binoculars, and spotting scopes on birds migrating through the area in the spring, on the way to breeding grounds in the far north. High-tech gear has made watching birds a close-up and personal experience in recent years.

The book's photographer and I were in town for the annual Potholes & Prairie Birding Festival. Such gatherings have become fixtures throughout the birding universe, often at locations where spring and fall migrations create avian traffic jams. Thousands of dedicated birders flock to these events every year. On some of these occasions, wind and weather conditions produce so-called fallouts or blowdowns of birds in vast numbers, creatures desperately seeking nourishment in preparation for, or in the aftermath of, daunting flights measured in the thousands of miles. When this occurs, the excitement among birders rivals New Year's Eve in Times Square. Typically, bird festivals feature birding gurus, ornithologists, bird writers and artists, and other wildlife experts who give talks and lead workshops on birding subjects both familiar and arcane, and who, most important for the attendees, conduct small groups on day-long expeditions in search of the birds in the vicinity, the rarer the species the better, and the more the merrier.

Our leader on this morning's jaunt was Julie Zickefoose, a former field biologist for The Nature Conservancy, a leading bird illustrator and watercolorist, and a familiar voice on National Public Radio, esteemed for her thoughtful commentaries on the delights and vagaries of the natural world.

A half hour from our lodgings, Julie directed the bus driver to turn off the highway onto a dirt road just as the light of dawn dimly illuminated the landscape for the birders, now eager to see what species this road would lead them to. It was in the low fifties, cold for June, and the leaden sky threatened to open up. The birders were ready for foul weather, which they called "fowl weather," with rain jackets, Windbreakers, hoodies, head scarves, and baseball caps, hiking shoes, boots, and wellies.

The bus came to a sudden stop next to a pond, one of numerous "potholes" left behind by the action of glaciers millennia ago. Together with rolling hills, prairie grasslands, wooded coulees, and cultivated fields, the potholes make central North Dakota a birding hot spot even in near frigid conditions.

ABOVE: An annual birding festival attracts enthusiasts to Carrington, North Dakota, from all over the country, for one of hundreds of events that bring bird experts and amateur bird watchers together to revel in the sight of finding and identifying dozens of species in a single weekend.

There are more than 800 species of birds in North America, and another 350 regional variations of particular species. Then there are the "accidentals," birds that belong in other regions of the world but somehow have landed in the United States. The average bird watcher is content to enjoy the spectacle of a very small percentage of the bird population. The extreme birder, for whom bird watching is more competition than a hobby, is a different story. This individual has a consuming passion for finding and identifying as many species as possible, whether in his or her own neighborhood or native state, or across the continent, or even the entire world. The passion is ramped up by the sheer volume of the winged creatures being targeted, as well as by their widely divergent appearance and behavior. It may be relatively easy to differentiate the dabblers from the divers among ducks, but it is another matter to know with certainty the differences great and small among warblers, say, or sparrows. The complexity of the genuses makes the study of birds rich beyond measure. If birds are "God's nervous system," as someone once observed, bird watchers are their EKG, electrified by each new discovery. You never know what's going to show up at your feeder, let alone in the wild.

"I'm going to try to call in a sora," said Julie in a low voice, a signal perhaps that we should all speak softly, if at all, during her experiment.

Porzana carolina, or sora, is a small rail with relatively long wings and tail, weighing 2.6 ounces. You could look it up, as I did, in *The Sibley Guide to Birds*. When the bird gives voice, it makes a high, squealing sound, which the guide's author, David Allen Sibley, describes as a whinny.

As Julie and an assistant crept down from the road toward the marsh, we followed their progress intently. They came to a halt and dropped into a crouch. The assistant pointed her iPod at the rushes and played the sora song: *ko-WEEeee-e-e-e, ee, ee* (lyrics by Sibley). The iPod operator waited a few moments, then played the song again.

No response. After a few more minutes of fruitless serenading with their iPod, Julie and her assistant came back to the group.

"Let's move on," Julie said. "Let's get dirty."

After we'd advanced several hundred yards along the dirt road, it began spitting rain. No one seemed to notice except me.

Julie led us to a barbed-wire fence at the edge of a vast pasture. She held strands of the wire apart, and we squeezed through single file. I brought up the rear.

"Watch out for cow pies and gopher holes," she told me with a smile.

In the distance, a herd of cattle, perhaps disturbed by an intrusion of some kind on their grazing range, bellowed in full throat. We picked our way through a field knee-high with grass and other botanical specimens.

"Look at the wildflowers," Julie declared, her voice vibrating with enthusiasm. "There's pussytoes," she said, kneeling to take notice and, a few steps later, kneeling again, "and wild penstemon . . . and that's some kind of gaillardia . . . and look, anemone . . . and scarlet globe mallow."

Serious birders like Julie Zickefoose view and study birds in the context of their natural surroundings. "Plant communities are the backbone for absolutely everything else I'm interested in," she has said.

Back in our own ecological niche, Julie pointed skyward and said, "Look what's coming." The birders swiveled their heads and lifted their binoculars in unison. "Marbled godwit!" someone cried as the bird in question alighted in the near distance. With its long beak and longish legs, the godwit is a denizen of coastal beaches and tidal flats, except during breeding season, when it flies to North Dakota for the Potholes & Prairie Birding Festival. I also learned that the godwit meant a lot to Lynne, a medical technologist who had driven four hundred miles from her home in Minnesota to attend the festival. "Lifer!" she cried after laying eyes on the bird. It was the first of sixteen life birds she would collect over the weekend. After photographing the godwit to post on her blog, Lynne exchanged high fives with another festival-goer named . . . Wren.

It continued to rain on and off, but spirits lifted as species after species presented themselves in our pasture, which a bit later on Julie called "this magic piece of land." Sightings, or "killer looks," as Julie called them, were made by one and all: a grasshopper sparrow on a post, a pair of western kingbirds on the barbed wire, a chestnut-collared longspur in flight, a clay-colored sparrow, which to me looked just like the grasshopper sparrow, and a savannah sparrow, which to me looked just like the clay-colored sparrow.

My education in birds was furthered, at least somewhat, by the kindness of strangers. Later it occurred to me that this was simply a manifestation of common birding etiquette, but whenever someone glommed onto a bird with a spotting scope, that person would announce it. "I've got a bobolink in the lens

ABOVE: While birds are the primary target for birders, all flora and fauna spur interest in people who are naturalists at heart. Bill Thompson III, editor of *Bird Watcher's Digest* and a frequent tour leader at the Potholes & Prairie festival, checks a field guide for confirmation of a waterfowl sighting.

ABOVE: The western kingbird is one of more than a hundred and fifty species spotted during a recent birding festival in central North Dakota. The bird, a member of the tyrant flycatcher family, migrates from its winter grounds in Mexico and Central America, favoring farmland and open country on its journey northward. OPPOSITE: Ordinary as it may appear, the Baird's sparrow is one of the most highly valued sightings during the spring migration in the Dakotas because it is such a shy, elusive species. Dwelling in high-grass prairies, the bird's best identifying marks are the ochre median stripe on the crown of its head and the dark spots on the neck.

if anyone's interested," a bearded fellow said, stepping away from his scope. Several birders were interested, myself included. When my turn came to peer through the scope, I was thrilled by the clarity and detail of the bird before my eyes. In breeding season, the male bobolink is mostly black, with streaks of white on the back and a pale yellow nape.

"It used to be called the skunk blackbird," the man volunteered. "Its song sounds a little like R2-D2, the chattering robot in *Star Wars*."

I looked at my watch. It was 6:45 a.m. The day was young. I had the feeling a staggering amount of birds awaited to be seen and counted. (In fact, Julie's group ended up identifying seventy-eight different species.) Birding was not for the short-attention-span crowd.

"All right," Julie was saying, "could we all coalesce and get ready for the Baird's? Anybody got the Baird's sparrow on their life list?" she asked.

Several hands shot up. The Baird's sparrow was a hard get, a furtive little bird of solitary habit, almost impossible to spot except in parts of North Dakota and neighboring Canada during the bird's breeding season, which was now.

More high fives were exchanged, moments later, when the speck of a bird finally came into view. Julie demonstrated a kind of dance, called "the life bird wiggle," to mark the discovery. Perching on a fence wire, the Baird's was captured in close-up on several spotting scopes. When I got a chance to look through one of the scopes, I saw a dark void. I must have sighed audibly, because the owner of the scope picked up on my disappointment.

"What's up? Oh, I see, you're getting nothing but coat." He called to the fellow standing between his scope and the target bird, "Hey, could you step to one side so we can see?"

The obstructing figure obliged, and the Baird's sparrow was there for me to see at last. To my uneducated eye it was just another sparrow—small beak, short tail, white breast, brownish wing feathers, and yet I knew how callous it was for me to dismiss the bird as I listened to the chorus of cheers around me. The Baird's sparrow was a precious acquisition for the life listers among us, and Julie was the hero who had brought it to them.

And so, in a remote fastness on the plains of North Dakota, "where if the wind stops blowing everyone falls down," I had witnessed the spectacle of bird watching at its best, and I had come to appreciate the essential, inimitable . . . looniness . . . of it all. But by the end of the day, like everyone else, I was birded out.

—LAURENCE SHEEHAN

INTRODUCTION

BIRD FESTIVALS SUCH AS THE ANNUAL POTHOLES & PRAIRIE
EXTRAVAGANZA IN NORTH DAKOTA, THE SNOW GOOSE
FESTIVAL OF THE PACIFIC FLYWAY IN CALIFORNIA, AND THE
FESTIVAL OF OWLS IN MINNESOTA ARE ONLY ONE MANIFES-
TATION OF AMERICA'S GROWING LOVE AFFAIR WITH BIRDS
AND BIRDING.

The U.S. Fish and Wildlife Service estimates that close to fifty million Americans watch, feed, and/or photograph birds every year. *The Birding Life* is an
effort to capture not just the experience of bird watching in all its insouciance,
diversity, and surprise, but also to show how devotees of the species reveal the
depths of their passion in their homes and haunts.

Images of birds are powerful and evocative almost beyond our ability to
express and to measure. Take the ineffable Peacock Room. Once the dining
room in the London home of a nineteenth-century shipping magnate, it now
stands reassembled and restored in all its glory in the Freer Gallery of Art in
Washington, D.C. Transformed into a harmony of blue and gold by the American-born artist, James Abbott McNeil Whistler, the room has shutters adorned
with golden peacocks, and its ceiling and leather-covered walls are painted in
their entirety with a pattern of peacock feathers. The *Chicago Tribune* called the
room "the world's greatest masterpiece of decorative art" when it first came to
these shores in 1904. Today more than ever, the Peacock Room represents our
desire to be surrounded by the beauty and luxury of birds, both real and
imagined.

The beauty of birding in real life is in the eye of the beholder, and it mostly happens not in far-flung locations in the world, but in our backyards and parks, on our beaches, rivers, and lakes, in our marshes and meadows, and even in our cemeteries and landfills. Robert Winkler, who writes frequently about birds, put his finger on the universal appeal of watching this unique species in action: "They are numerous, diverse, intelligent, talkative, and beautiful; their power of flight never ceases to amaze; and they're the most conspicuous class of wild animal—even in the suburbs, they're just about everywhere."

In *The Birding Life*, we'll venture into the field to see birders in their most natural habitat: watching birds in the wild. Then we'll follow these dedicated birders and other avian enthusiasts back to their own homes. Here, birds are a recurring theme in paintings and watercolors, in folk art and antiques, in sculptures and carvings, in textiles and rugs, in collections and ceramics, and in just about anything else that invites the graceful touch of design.

In Part I, "Birders in Birdland," we meet the iconic figures, from Audubon to Peterson to Sibley, who discovered and documented America's native birds for the general public. We'll befriend a Texas couple who work tirelessly to preserve wild country vital to the survival of native birds, at the same time filling their ranch home with bird images executed by native artists. We'll meet two New Yorkers, one a schoolboy, the other a self-described "urban archaeologist," who chase their birds in Central Park. We'll peer over the shoulder of an amateur ornithologist whose journals document years of travel in pursuit of birds, illustrated with his own exquisitely rendered images of species both plain

Homeowners find numerous ways to bring their enthusiasm for birds into their own nests, including this avian collection arrayed on a fireplace mantel in the Maine house of Sharon and Paul Mrozinski. Nineteenth-century lithographs of eggs surmount framed images of birds in various styles.

and exotic. We'll sail to a remote Maine island where the Atlantic puffin is king and the spirit of Audubon has cast its magic spell for more than seven decades. And we'll visit the farm of an Ohio family who have made a career of birding and even built a tower the better to see the birds.

In Part II, "Bird Houses," among many stops we'll visit the home of a lifelong sportsman and conservationist with one of the finest collections of Audubon prints and bird carvings in private hands. We'll go behind the scenes at one of the nation's most important scientific collections of birds, nests, and eggs. (It is interesting to note that while collecting eggs, nests, and even birds was a popular activity in the Victorian era, today there are strict limits on the practice.) And we'll visit the studios of two artists who draw on birds for inspiration for their highly original work.

In Part III, "At Home with Birds," we'll visit locales where decorating with an avian theme flies to new heights, including the Brooklyn loft of two young sisters with a hipster take on the natural world, the New England farmhouse of a ceramics artist whose pieces depict birds with a combination of sophistication and whimsy, and a winter retreat where a diverse collection of carved shorebirds looks out upon their living counterparts in the Florida Keys.

Finally, in "Birding Resources," we'll provide hundreds of useful sources of information and inspiration for bird watchers of every level of interest.

Birds have triumphed against all odds in a world full of natural and human-created hazards to their health and very existence, thanks in part to the artists and conservationists who have taken up their cause. As *The Birding Life* demonstrates, birds have also made their presence felt in the homes of enthusiasts, in the form of warm, comfortable, and eclectic living spaces—nests fit for the most regal of birds, and birders.

OPPOSITE: America's centuries-old tradition of bird carving has a place of honor in this painted cupboard in the Connecticut home of Donal O'Brien. Golden plovers atop the cupboard and on its bottom shelf were made in Nantucket in about 1840 to 1850. Among the duck decoys is a prized red-breasted merganser made on Long Island in about 1950. ABOVE: Portraits of birds, which continue to play a role in avian science, are also esteemed for their beauty, as in this study of a bird in flight made by artist Virginia S. Precourt in preparation for executing a larger work.

PART I
BIRDERS IN BIRDLAND

Watch bird watchers watch birds in their favorite habitats in city, suburb, and countryside. More than the stuff of dreams, birding is a ritual driven by affection, curiosity, and respect for nature and wildlife in all its forms. Yet it is the simplest of diversions. Question: "Favorite bird?" Birder's answer: "The one I just saw."

Night hawk, with female. Wilson called the hawk "a bird perpendicular...

ORIGIN OF THE SPECIES: TRAILBLAZING BIRDERS

SINCE THE EARLY NINETEENTH CENTURY, A HANDFUL OF ARTISTS AND NATURALISTS HAVE SERVED AS THE FAITHFUL INTERPRETERS OF THE WILD BIRDS OF AMERICA. THEY HAVE BEEN INORDINATELY HELPFUL GUIDES FOR THE MASS OF ORDINARY BIRD WATCHERS, ASTUTE OBSERVERS FOR THE PROFESSIONAL STUDENTS OF ORNITHOLOGY AND RELATED SCIENCES, AND, FOR EACH OTHER, INSTIGATORS IF NOT ACTUAL INSPIRATIONS OF BIGGER AND BETTER WORK IN THEIR CHOSEN FIELD. TAKING MEASURE OF THE ACCOMPLISHMENTS OF THESE ICONIC FIGURES WILL ALSO HELP US TO GRASP THE LARGER STORY OF BIRD WATCHING IN AMERICA.

The creation of America's avian iconography got off to a bumpy start when two young men of artistic bent arrived in the New World within ten years of each other. With few friends, limited means, and the vaguest of personal ambitions, one day each elected to pursue an impossible dream—to paint and describe all the birds of America.

The first to arrive was Alexander Wilson, a weaver, peddler, and poet who emigrated from western Scotland in 1794. As a young man, he was described as having an ascetic aspect, with a hooked nose, high cheekbones, and a burning expression in his eyes. There is no doubt about his tenacity. Beginning in 1804,

Wilson traveled ten thousand miles throughout the fledgling nation of the United States, on foot and by boat, compiling color portraits of some 262 birds, including 48 species never before identified. His *American Ornithology: The Natural History of the Birds of the United States* appeared in nine volumes, published from 1808 to 1814.

The second figure to dominate avian culture in early America was John James Audubon, the son of a French naval officer and his chambermaid mistress. John James came to the United States from France in 1803, primarily to dodge Napoleon's military draft. Audubon was fascinated with birds from an early age, but it was not until he was in his forties that he raised enough money, on a tour of England and Scotland, to undertake publishing his magnum opus.

Birds of America was compiled over a period of eighteen years. The finished product contains 435 hand-colored, life-size prints of 497 bird species, made from engraved copper plates. In addition to the sheer artistry of "the greatest picture book ever produced," as one critic would call it, the double elephant folio (26.5 by 39 inches) was scaled to impress. For instance, the first plate, depicting a wild turkey, was more than ten times larger than the turkey shown in Wilson's *American Ornithology*. In 2010, a double elephant folio in pristine condition fetched $10 million at auction in London.

WILSON AND AUDUBON: EARLY YEARS

The reticent Wilson and the ebullient Audubon were contrasting personalities, but they shared a consuming interest in birds. They were both crack shots, and killing birds for study was a prerequisite before the invention of binoculars and cameras. In their embrace of the American wilderness, with all its dangers and delights, they also personified the pioneering spirit that shaped nineteenth-century life in the New World.

Settling in the Philadelphia area, Wilson scraped by in a variety of teaching jobs. He had a particular interest in the natural world, but it was not until he met William Bartram, son of the botanist John Bartram, that Wilson became obsessed with birds. Bartram opened his father's extensive library to the young man, urged him to study birds, and encouraged him to develop his talent for drawing and painting birds. In 1804, Wilson embarked on the project to locate, paint, and describe every bird species in America. There were believed to be some 340 species in the United States of his time, so in the end he fell about 80 birds short, no mean achievement nevertheless.

PRECEDING PAGES: Alexander Wilson is known as the father of American ornithology because he was the first to explore the American wilderness with the goal of identifying, drawing, and describing all the birds of the New World. He published nine volumes of his *American Ornithology* from 1808 to 1814, illustrating 268 species, including 48 which had never been described before. ABOVE: Wilson grouped three or more birds on each engraved plate, with eight to nine plates per volume. The framed prints are in the collection of Maine artist and antiques dealer John Sideli.

Wilson traveled as much in search of funding as in the pursuit of birds. The high cost of engraving forced him to sell subscriptions to each volume even as he was in the midst of preparing it. President Thomas Jefferson subscribed to the entire set in 1807, while still in the White House, based on a prospectus Wilson had mailed him.

On a trip west to drum up sales in 1810, Wilson set forth in a rowboat down the Allegheny River. He painted *The Ornithologist* on its stern, prompting a fellow traveler to ask if the odd name referred to a tribe of Indians. In Louisville, at loose ends because no one had answered his letters of introduction, Wilson noticed a newspaper ad claiming that one J. J. Audubon was available to give lessons in drawing and to paint portraits "that would be good likenesses." Wilson decided to call on the fellow.

Audubon had arrived in Louisville in circuitous fashion. Following a slave rebellion in Santo Domingo, now Haiti, in 1788, Audubon's father had decided to sell his sugar plantation and return with his children to the relative safety of France. With his birth name of Jean-Jacques Audubon, the boy enjoyed a pampered existence with his stepmother at her estate near Nantes, learning to play the flute, dance, ride, and fence. He loved to walk in the woods, often returning with birds' nests and eggs, which he would draw on paper. His father encouraged the boy's interest in nature. "He would point out the elegant movement of the birds," Audubon later recalled in his journal, "and the beauty and softness of their plumage. He called my attention to their show of pleasure or sense of danger, their perfect forms and splendid attire."

In 1803, the senior Audubon obtained a passport for his son in the anglicized name of John James Audubon and sent him to the United States to lay claim to Mill Grove, an 284-acre estate near Philadelphia, which his father had purchased with proceeds from the sale of his sugar plantation.

"Hunting, fishing, drawing, and music occupied my every moment," Audubon wrote of his time at Mill Grove. "Cares I knew not, and cared naught about them." He made a close study of the birds found on the estate, with an eye toward illustrating them in a realistic style not yet seen in avian art.

"I shot the first kingfisher I met," Audubon wrote in his Mill Grove journal,

OPPOSITE: The John James Audubon Center at Mill Grove in Pennsylvania re-creates the studio where Audubon began drawing birds with serious intent. He also mastered taxidermy here, which helped him to arrange his subject birds in the dramatic postures for which his work is noted. ABOVE: "Brown Pelican" appears in Mill Grove's four-volume elephant folio of Audubon's masterwork, *The Birds of America*.

PLATE 28

ABOVE: As a young naturalist, Roger Tory Peterson turned to silhouettes to help bird watchers identify species by their anatomical profiles. In his best-selling field guides, Peterson called attention to the physical features of birds, or field marks, that could also be used reliably for identification.

"pierced the body with wire, fixed it to the board, another wire held the head, smaller ones fixed the feet . . . there stood before me the real kingfisher. I outlined the bird, colored it. This was my first drawing actually from nature."

When Mill Grove failed to provide Audubon the income he had anticipated, he moved west and opened a dry goods store in Louisville. It was here that the two bird enthusiasts finally met on March 19, 1810. Wilson introduced himself and showed off Volume I and Volume II of *American Ornithology.* Then Wilson detailed the terms on which the books were sold. Audubon drew out a pen and was about to sign a purchase agreement for $120 when, as Audubon recalled many years later, his business partner called an admonishment from the back of the store: "That's a lot to pay, especially since you know more about birds and paint birds better than this fellow."

The remark gave Audubon pause, and he decided not to support Wilson's work-in-progress. In a life-changing moment, Audubon saw for the first time that he had the talent as an artist and naturalist, and the skills and strength as a woodsman to create his own visual census of the birds of the New World.

KING PENGUIN

If John James Audubon introduced a revolutionary sense of realism to the world of birding, Roger Tory Peterson was vital in giving birders a virtually foolproof system for identifying birds. Arguably the most influential naturalist of the twentieth century, Peterson and his field guides converted more Americans to bird watching than did any other single phenomenon. While he greatly admired Audubon, and wrote frequent paeans to his work, Peterson was also in thrall to Louis Agassiz Fuertes, an ornithologist and artist who illustrated birds and mammals in more than sixty books in the early part of the century.

"My own life's work was sparked by a Fuertes color plate, a blue jay that my seventh-grade teacher, Miss Blanche Hornbeck, gave me to copy," Peterson once recalled. While from Audubon's art he gained a sense of design and space, from Fuertes he learned how a bird was put together, "the personality of the species."

Toward the end of his life, Peterson, or King Penguin as he was known affectionately, sometimes lamented his failure to dedicate as much time and energy to "easel painting" as he had committed to other activities. Yet his book, *A Field Guide to the Birds, Giving Field Marks of All Species Found in Eastern North America,* first published in 1934, was startlingly original. "The style he introduced of focusing down on the diagnostic traits of each species and indicating

them with a clear field mark was brilliant," wrote scientist E. O. Wilson. In the second edition of the guide, Peterson introduced another revolutionary teaching device: seventy-seven silhouettes of the most commonly seen birds, showing how easy it is to tell birds by their shapes and postures, regardless of field marks.

TODAY'S BIRDING GURUS

Peterson influenced the lives and careers of many individuals, including two of today's most prominent field guide authors, Kenn Kaufman and David Allen Sibley.

"The other boys in my neighborhood idolized baseball players or movie cowboys," says Kaufman, "but my hero was Roger Tory Peterson." Kaufman was especially taken with *Wild America,* a chronicle of a 30,000-mile automobile trip Peterson made around the country in 1953.

ABOVE: Mill Grove, the Pennsylvania farmhouse where John James Audubon developed his skills as a painter and naturalist from 1804 to 1808, was built in 1762 and today serves as an Audubon nature center. FOLLOWING PAGES: Birds both drawn and mounted are on display in the studio at Mill Grove, as well as birds' eggs collected like a string of pearls. The murals in the house were painted in the 1950s and depict species and places Audubon witnessed during his career.

"That book became my daily passport to the wilderness," Kaufman once remarked. One passing notation in particular caught his eye: the fact that Peterson's list of birds sighted in 1953 had totaled 572 species: "That anyone should see the great majority of birds that normally lived in North America (over 800) in a single year seemed almost unbelievable."

In retrospect, Peterson's journey, though unplanned as such, was the original birding "big year," and Kaufman sought to emulate it in 1973. He dropped out of high school and set forth from his Kansas home to hitchhike across America in search of birds. Later, he figured out that his wanderings covered 69,000 miles. (Perhaps more amazing, he spent less than $1,000 the whole time.)

Kaufman did Peterson more than one better that year. He saw 666 species. Yet by the end of 1973, the total number itself did not really matter. On his trip Kaufman had grown from a boy to a young man with a newly confirmed sense of self. Like his hero, he would build a career in birding, espousing conservation and educating people about the importance of nature and the environment. His Kaufman Field Guide series took advantage of new technology to depict birds with computer-enhanced color photography. Like Peterson, who once described brown pelicans as "seriocomic" and called African vultures "the undertakers of the plains," Kaufman is a vivid writer. He has compared flamingos, for example, to "lanky javelins . . . creatures left over from some prehistoric experiment with flight."

David Allen Sibley, son of ornithologist Fred Sibley, aspired to write and illustrate a field guide to birds from an early age, but it was not until he met Roger Tory Peterson that he began to believe he could actually pull off such a thing.

"It was the early 1970s, and I was twelve," Sibley relates. "A friend of my father's, Noble Proctor, taught ornithology at Southern Connecticut State University. He knew Peterson well and arranged for me to meet him at his studio. It was just following the Old Lyme Christmas Bird Count in which both Noble and Roger had taken part."

Fred Sibley, who was head of Yale's bird collection at the time, did not think his son's career ambitions were unrealistic. "But to see Roger in person," David points out, "in that place where he drew birds and painted birds, made me realize someone could actually make a living doing bird guides. Roger was living proof it was possible."

Sibley already had considerable hands-on experience with birds. When he was seven, his father, then the director of Point Reyes Bird Observatory in California, frequently brought David to the research station to work with him.

"A lot of the work at the research station back then was banding birds," Sibley relates, "and I was allowed to help until I got quite proficient at it. Holding live birds helped me appreciate the variations among species—the heavier weight and the more pronounced musculature of the downy woodpecker, compared to the chickadee, for example, and how the woodpecker pounded you with its bill if you weren't careful!"

Like Kaufman, David Sibley was not cut out for a conventional education. He dropped out of Cornell before finishing freshman year, "because everything I wanted to do was based on field work, not classroom study." He drove throughout America in a Ford van retrofitted with a camp bed and a makeshift kitchen. For eleven years, beginning in 1988, he supported himself by working as a guide for a birding tour company fifty to sixty days a year. The income freed him up to spend the rest of the year watching birds on his own, making sketches of them and taking notes on their songs, calls, plumage, and behaviors.

"From the beginning of my travels, I collected material for my 'field guide,'" Sibley observes, "but it wasn't until I was five or six years into the research that I actually told people what I was working on."

When *The Sibley Guide to Birds* was published in 2000, with the sponsorship of the National Audubon Society, it was an instant success. It described 810 species and contained more than 6,600 illustrations. It improved on earlier guides in various ways, perhaps most importantly by including drawings of all the birds in multiple plumages and in flight. Critics have remarked on "the warmth and exactitude" of Sibley's drawing style.

Sibley's field guides rely on artwork to depict birds, while Kaufman's guides use photographs. "Our two books are really complementary," Sibley observes. "The bottom line is," he adds, articulating a mission that began with Audubon and Wilson, "both of us are just trying to get people excited about birds and to bring more people into birding."

OPPOSITE: Two leading field guide authors in today's birding community are Kenn Kaufman (top), now based in Ohio, and David Sibley, who lives and works in Massachusetts. ABOVE: While Kaufman's books depend on color photographs to show birds, Sibley uses finely detailed drawings. Both naturalists developed their knowledge of the avian world through extensive travels and close observations of bird behavior.

WHERE THE BIRDS ARE:
TEXAS HILL COUNTRY

T HE TOWERING GATE WELCOMING VISITORS TO BUCK-
HOLLOW RANCH IN CONCAN, TEXAS, FEATURES A WHITE-
TAIL DEER ON ONE SIDE AND A WILD TURKEY AND A BOBWHITE
QUAIL ON THE OTHER. THE WILDLIFE THEME COULD NOT BE
MORE APPROPRIATE FOR JAN AND JACK CATO'S 6,000-ACRE
SPREAD OF LIMESTONE HILLS, CLIFFS, AND VALLEYS IN THE
HEART OF TEXAS HILL COUNTRY.

Although their primary residence, Houston, is not exactly known for its conservationist ethic, the Catos are. They have been nurturing their land back to its natural state for more than a decade, and in 2004 the Texas Parks and Wildlife Department bestowed a Lone Star Steward Award on Jack Cato for his efforts.

"We don't have cattle or crops, and we like it that way," says Jack. "We are a wildlife ranch."

Spring is especially wild—with birds—at Buckhollow. From April through June, more than two hundred species, both migrating and nesting varieties, may be seen here, as well as countless butterflies and dragonflies, flights of cave-dwelling bats by the hundreds, and spectacular displays of wildflowers. Two endangered birds that are always welcome sights are the black-capped vireo and the golden-cheeked warbler, species that breed only in the Hill Country. Along with two other birds, the zone-tailed hawk and the green kingfisher, they comprise the Texas Grand Slam that competitive birders strive to see in a single year.

PRECEDING PAGES: Above the fireplace adjacent to the kitchen hangs a 1960's pencil and watercolor curlew by Kermit Oliver, artist and postal clerk in Waco, Texas. Shown in photos on the mantel, the black-capped vireo and the golden-cheeked warbler are endangered species that breed in this part of the Hill Country. ABOVE: At the ranch, Jack Cato sizes up the flyway with a spotting scope, while Jan Cato looks for birds along the Dry Frio River. RIGHT: The canvas swan decoy on the Lazy Susan dining table was made by East Coast carver Madison Mitchell in about 1950. A folk curlew with a bill fashioned from a pitchfork tine occupies a niche in the limestone river rock wall, over a saddle presented as the "All-Around Cowboy" award in the Cuero Youth Rodeo of 1970; Kermit Oliver painted the sandhill crane over the colorfully tiled fireplace.

A SMALL BIRDING MARVEL

A must-stop for birders in Texas Hill Country is Neal's Dining Room in the town of Concan, ninety miles west of San Antonio. The building is made of the same limestone rocks used to build Jan and Jack Cato's Buckhollow Ranch. Hummingbird feeders are set up at practically every window. The eatery overlooks the cypress-lined Frio River, which follows its wandering course several hundred feet below the outdoor terrace. *Texas Highways* magazine called it "one of the most spectacular spots in the state . . . a small marvel that time has overlooked."

Neal's Dining Room has chicken fried steak and fried pickles on the menu, and Blue Bell ice cream, a Texas staple, for dessert. It has smiling waitresses. It's the place where the Hill Country's most respected bird guides bring their birders for lunch after exploring the miles of trails along and around the river. Beneath the chalkboard menu is a comprehensive bird list for the Concan area, which birders inscribe with daily sightings by species and viewing location.

The restaurant is across the street from Neal's Vacation Lodges, founded in 1926 by local rancher Tom Neal and his wife, Vida Thrift Neal. Adjacent is Neal's Store, stocked with groceries, ice, gifts, and souvenirs. On offer are bird field lists to acquaint oneself with the local avian population, bird earrings, and other small gifts and souvenirs of this birding hotspot.

ABOVE: Sturdy, cowboy-scale bunk beds built by workers from the Civilian Conservation Corps in the 1930s, are as good as new today. OPPOSITE, ABOVE: The Hermès scarf designed by Kermit Oliver celebrates Texas wildlife both domestic and wild, including a magnificent tom turkey. Oliver is the sole American artist to receive a commission from the famed French fashion purveyor. OPPOSITE, BELOW: Brightening the bedside table in the bunkroom are wildflowers in an improvised vase and a nest found on the ranch that had outlived its usefulness.

Conservation of indigenous species of all kinds is central to the Catos' mission at the ranch. "Years ago we were on another ranch as visitors," Jan recalls. "The owner had just ordered the extermination of red ants on his property, even though the ants are the main food supply for Texas's famous horny toads, which are themselves endangered. That's when we realized we wanted to own our own land—to control the farming and ranching practices that have been detrimental to the environment."

The ranch house itself might be described as a study in Bunkhouse Chic, with regional art and artifacts setting the tone, including a saddle awarded as the All-Around Cowboy prize in the 1970 Cuero Youth Rodeo, and a framed hand-screened silk Hermès scarf designed with a wild-turkey motif by Texas artist Kermit Oliver. The house was built in the 1930s by skilled stonemasons and other craftsmen recruited from the Civilian Conservation Corps (CCC). One of the CCC's Depression-era projects had been Garner State Park, a 1,400-acre sanctuary not far from Concan. Buckhollow's main residence and water tower were constructed in the same style as the park buildings, using limestone rocks gathered from riverbeds and hand-forged iron door straps and hinges. A traditional woven-wire cedar fence runs along the house on the front side. The original owner, a Humble Oil engineer, oriented the house toward the southeast, to take advantage of prevailing winds in the era before air-conditioning.

Inside, the spacious central room has river rock walls and two colorfully tiled corner fireplaces with fire screens with figures of deer and mantels decked with canvas duck decoys and carvings of East Coast shorebirds that migrate to Texas in winter. Day of the Dead images from Mexico hang throughout, and Oriental rugs are scattered on the tile floors. A wagon wheel wired to serve as a rustic chandelier is suspended over a classic Texas ranch dining room set, on whose lazy Susan floats a canvas swan decoy. Two bedroom suites flank the main room, each with four bunks rugged enough for Texas rangers and with large casement windows that flood the room with light by day.

Since acquiring Buckhollow in 1997, the Catos have cleared brush, including invasive ash juniper, with controlled burns on 1,800 acres, although some brush is left in piles to provide cover for skunks and armadillos. (The armadillo is another quintessential Texas critter in decline because of habitat destruction.) A spidery network of dirt roads allows Jan to cruise the ranch on her Honda four-by-four with her dog, Champ, at her side. She always carries snippers, to cut sprigs of ash juniper, and binoculars, to sight cedar waxwings in the pink chokeberry (a desirable native plant species) and bluebirds at the

ABOVE: Having built and erected some 150 bluebird houses throughout the ranch property, Jack Cato conducts occasional inspections to see if his efforts have borne fruit. Five eggs is a typical output for mating bluebirds in the spring. ABOVE RIGHT: Jan Cato takes Champ on the Honda 4 x 4 to chase birds and check habitat on the six thousand acres of Buck Hollow Ranch in the Texas Hill Country, west of San Antonio.

more than 150 houses Jack has erected for that species. At an overlook, she'll stop to watch young redtail hawks learning to fly on the thermal winds swirling by the limestone cliffs.

"Even if I'm just walking from house to garage, I always have my binoculars," says Jan, whose favorite sighting is the black-backed lesser goldfinch, a form unique to Texas, "with a playful-sounding call they use to talk to each other." Jan also regularly scopes out the eastern phoebes in the clay nests they build under the eaves of the house, the painted buntings and blue grosbeaks at her poolside feeders, and the golden-fronted woodpeckers dining on her custom-mixed suet.

While Jan and Jack Cato relish the experience of "living in another world" every time they come to Buckhollow, the conservation goals of the ranch remain paramount. Federally licensed banders set up shop every spring at the ranch, banding some 350 birds, mostly black-chinned hummers, over a two-day span. Volunteers also band birds at the Gulf Coast Bird Observatory in Lake Jackson, near Houston, for which Jan serves as a board member. The group was formed to preserve the shrinking birding habitat along the Texas coast.

"As more oil refineries, boat marinas, and beach houses take over the land along the coast," Jan observes, "migrating birds have less and less habitat to call their own. And when migrating birds go into decline here, because of habitat loss, they go into decline all over the country."

The Dry Frio River can flood its banks or run underground, depending on a particular year's rainfall, but it is an important habitat for birds and other wild creatures in all seasons. Along with the hills, meadows, and woodlands the river supports some 135 species of native and migrant birds. In this part of Texas, sighting a golden-cheeked warbler, zonetail hawk, black-capped vireo, and green kingfisher in one season constitutes the coveted Hill Country Grand Slam for birders.

BIRDBOY'S URBAN AERIE

WOOIP, WOOIP, WOOIP ISN'T THE LATEST TRACK OF AN INDIE ROCK BAND BUT TO THIRTEEN-YEAR-OLD ALEXANDER GOTTDIENER, IT'S THE CALL OF THE WILD—THE SONG OF A MALE LONG-EARED OWL LOOKING FOR COMPANY.

"It was one o'clock in the morning," relates Alexander. "I heard the owl before I saw it, which was really amazing," he says. "It woke my dad up, too. It was that loud."

What's perhaps more amazing is that Alexander, whose e-mail name is "Birdboy," saw the owl from his bedroom window in the middle of the urban wilds of Manhattan. "We have a lot of trees in the yard, and they provide cover for birds. I've seen more than fifty species from my window."

Owls are Alexander's favorite bird species, "so different from other birds," he says, "nocturnal, with unusual digestive systems, flat faces, and amazing eyes that look almost human." He keeps *Owls of the World,* one of many ornithology books he has collected, on his night table. Alexander's interest extends to other raptors, too, and he has passed New York State's challenging examination for qualifying as a licensed falconer.

Maria and Noah Gottdiener were quick to note and encourage their son's love of wild creatures, even tolerating the boy's early fascination with snakes, which served as his introduction to the natural world. He began collecting them from the woods and meadows surrounding the family's country home in upstate New York. Even today he maintains a menagerie that includes fifteen snakes and assorted turtles, lizards, and frogs. He and his younger sister, Genny, pick up and handle the creatures with aplomb. "Love me. Love my snakes," reads an inscription on a pillow in his bedroom in the city.

Alexander was first smitten with a bird at the age of nine. "I saw this bird picking its way through the grass near our house in the country," he recalls. "I studied it through binoculars. It was fairly large, with a gray head, yellow breast, and long legs. I went straight to the library, picked out a field guide, and identified it as a Connecticut warbler. I liked that it was rare. That warbler is what got me started in the field."

Outdoor enthusiasts, Alexander's parents plan vacations to educate their children about the wonders of the natural world. Birding expeditions to Costa Rica and Peru have provided Alexander with vivid experiences. "In one little preserve in Manu, Peru, live a thousand and seven species of birds," he relates, "and I saw forty in one visit." The highlight of the family's trip down the Amazon River was witnessing great flocks of macaws and parrots fly up to clay cliffs.

Closer to home, Alexander is a frequent visitor to Central Park. He often stops by on his way home from classes at the Browning School, to check on the spring and fall migrations of warblers and other species. He records his sightings in notebooks and is teaching himself to draw birds as well, emulating his birding heroes, Kenn Kaufman, David Sibley, and Roger Tory Peterson.

One day his mother took him to an art auction to see the Audubon prints that were up for sale. "They were beautiful but very expensive," Alexander relates. "She gave me a surprise present of a print of an eagle. It wasn't even my birthday, but she said it was Alexander Day." The eagle print, his most prized possession, hangs over his bed—for now. "I'm definitely taking it to college with me," he declares.

PRECEDING PAGES: The journal of a budding naturalist is open to two New York sightings and closely observed details about each bird, including the flycatcher's size ("HUGE!!!"). OPPOSITE, ABOVE: Alexander has sighted more than fifty species from his bedroom window alone. OPPOSITE, BELOW: Stuffed animals and a stately Audubon eagle, a gift from Mom, are welcome roommates. ABOVE: Maria and Noah Gottdiener join Alexander and his sister, Genny, in a birding dry run in the living room of their East Side home. FOLLOWING PAGES: The young teenager's already substantial ornithological library shows off some of his increasingly sophisticated artistic output. The appearance, calls, and nocturnal behavior of owls make that species Alexander's favorite, followed closely by snakes.

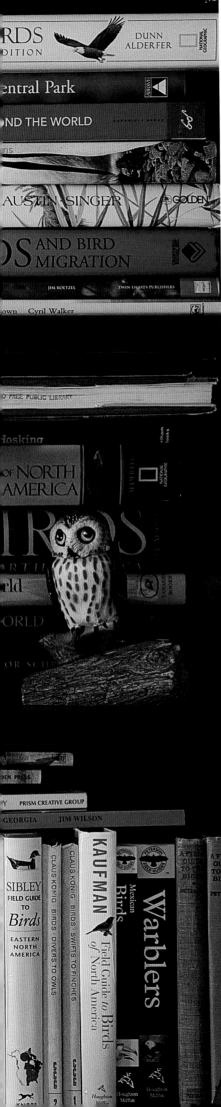

ALEXANDER'S TIPS FOR BEGINNING BIRDERS

ESSENTIAL GEAR

BACKPACK: "Mine is an old Abercrombie's knapsack."

PENS, PENCILS, AND NOTEPADS: "For sketching what I see."

FIELD GUIDES: "Pack different ones for different regions."

BINOCULARS: "Even though mine are large, they are efficient and portable."

SNACKS: Cheddar cheese, energy bars, fruit, crackers, bottled water

FAVORITE WEBSITES

AVIAN REVIEW: For birders and for those interested in reading or collecting books about birds. (http://sites.google.com/site/avianreview/)

BIRDGUIDES.COM: British site devoted to European and American birds; produces videos, books, and computer software for bird watchers. Slogan is "Better birding through technology."

FAVORITE MOVIE

My Side of the Mountain, based on a novel by Jean Craighead George about a boy and his falcon.

FIELD TIPS

MEMORIZE BIRD CALLS: "I like the identiFlyer," an electronic gadget that displays the name and picture of the bird as it plays its song.

BE PATIENT: "If you're in the right habitat, you'll see birds if you wait long enough."

LOOK FOR CLUES: "Learn to identify species by the tracks they leave and the feathers they shed."

TALK TO THE EXPERTS: "Staff members at wildlife reserves will point you in the right direction."

A WALK IN THE PARK
WITH BIRDING BOB

FOR SHEER ENTERTAINMENT VALUE IN NEW YORK CITY, YOU CAN'T GET MORE BANG FOR THE BUCK, OR BIRD FOR THE BUCK, THAN ON A SUNDAY MORNING STROLL THROUGH CENTRAL PARK WITH THE MAN KNOWN AS BIRDING BOB.

With a PhD in evolutionary biology and an encyclopedic knowledge of the flora and fauna of New York City, Robert DeCandido is the ideal leader for the three-hour bird watching walks that depart on any given Sunday at 9:00 a.m. from the dock on Turtle Pond, at approximately 79th Street in the center of the park. And the price is right: a mere $10 a head.

"We try to have fun," says the Bronx-born DeCandido, whose affable, low-key personality sets the tone for excursions through Central Park's favorite birding spots, from the Ramble to the Shakespeare Garden, from Belvedere Castle to Strawberry Fields. "The atmosphere is friendly and informal. We have many regulars, but newcomers of all abilities are always welcome." There's a collegial feeling among Bob's birders that is unmistakable. "The bird walks have become a kind of mobile community, and lifelong friendships have resulted."

Some 235 species of birds winter in Central Park, visit New York City during the spring and fall migrations, or live there year-round. But Bob tells his birders not to focus on the big picture. "We encourage people to think small," he says, "and look where no one else is looking."

Quintessential New York moments inevitably occur on the walks. Toward the end of one unusually warm Sunday in May, people were hot and tired, but game to press on. Presently the group of about fifteen gathered under the tallest tree in the Ramble, a spectacular tulip poplar with giant yellow-orange flowers. As birds emerged from the flowers, where they had been feeding on nectar and insects, Bob pointed out indigo buntings, scarlet tanagers, rose-breasted grosbeaks, and orchard orioles to his excited followers. "Then somebody's cell phone went off," DeCandido recalls, "and we all heard the ring tone—Beethoven's 'Ode to Joy.'"

Bob's partner, the noted bird and nature photographer Deborah Allen, joins him on most Sunday walks in the park and also assists on field trips and research projects. She is as patient and laid-back with the birders as he is. A walk she led one day in the fall began with twenty minutes of driving rain, but when the weather cleared, there was a giddy procession of sightings—northern parulas, magnolia warblers, three ovenbirds, "and some nice looks at an eastern wood-peewee, a male scarlet tanager, and a red-breasted nuthatch."

As an academic, Birding Bob has published studies on peregrine falcons, nesting owls, and American kestrels, and he has conducted research on bird migration in Nepal, Malaysia, Thailand, Spain, Turkey, and Israel. A paper he and Deborah coauthored on kestrels in Manhattan identified the locations of twenty-five nesting pairs on the island. Virtually all the pairs chose for their nesting sites the metal cornices of nineteenth-century buildings, at heights ranging from 40 to 125 feet above street level. Most sleek new skyscrapers don't offer niches so conducive to nesting.

Nocturnal bird watching reaches a new high when Bob and Deborah bring birders to the open-air deck on the Empire State Building. "It is one of the few places in the world where people are able to see migrating birds at night, and hear their calls as well," says Bob. On one recent ascent, birders identified over two hundred migrants from among the many thousands of birds that flew by the top of the building.

"New York City is my laboratory," DeCandido observed in a plea for urban biodiversity published in the *New York State Conservationist.* "When spring peepers begin chorusing in March, I am transformed from sleepy bookworm into mad scientist, keen to identify every plant and animal I find in my travels through Central Park."

PRECEDING PAGES: With the urban skyline of New York's West Side looming in the distance, Sunday morning birders enjoy the best that Central Park has to offer, including birds of all kinds in every season. OPPOSITE: Robert DeCandido and Deborah Allen lead birders of all levels of experience on Sunday morning tours of the park in search of the hundreds of species who live in the area or pass through it during migrations. Many participants are serious enough about the outings to take detailed notes on their sightings. ABOVE: The inspiring bronze statue "The Falconer," made in 1875 by English sculptor George Blackall Simonds, overlooks the bypass road at Seventy-second Street. It was restored in 1995 after incurring major damage by vandals.

OPPOSITE: Belvedere Castle, designed in 1875 as a Victorian Folly for Central Park, is a favorite spot for "Birding Bob" and his merry band of bird watchers. ABOVE: Birds photographed by Deborah Allen in the park include an adult male scarlet tanager in the park's Ramble during spring migration in mid-May (top left), a cedar waxwing feeding in a hawthorn near the Boathouse in mid-December (center left), and a drake hooded merganser, a winter dweller in the park, found at the Reservoir with a crawfish it had just caught (bottom left). The eastern screech owl (right), this one at its nest high in a tree, had declined in numbers in Central Park but its population is now on the rebound, thanks in part to efforts by Robert DeCandido.

JOURNAL
of Vincent A Sideli
1 · 9 · 7 · 8

DIARY OF A MAD BIRDER

VINCENT AND CAROL SIDELI ARE AS PASSIONATE ABOUT THEIR GARDENS AS THEY ARE ABOUT BIRDS. A RUFOUS-SIDED TOWHEE CAUGHT THEIR EYE AT A FEEDER IN 1966 AND THEY HAVE BEEN WATCHING BIRDS EVER SINCE. "I THOUGHT THAT TOWHEE WAS SO SPECTACULAR," RECALLS VINCE, "THAT I WENT OUT AND BOUGHT MY FIRST FIELD GUIDE."

Although the two schoolteachers, now retired, have traveled the world in pursuit of birds, from Machu Picchu to the Galapagos Islands, their most precious sanctuary may be their own backyard in Connecticut. Trees, shrubs, vines, and flowers make the yard an excellent habitat for New England's native birds and for seasonal migrants alike.

Over the years, the Sidelis have planted 50 clematis vines and 450 spring- and summer-flowering daylilies. Vince has seen ruby-throated hummingbirds sipping water from the lilies following a rainstorm, and tree frogs waiting to pounce on insects. With their promise of nectar, butterfly bushes and trumpet vines beckon to the hummers, as does a fragrant white-flowering hosta variety. The berries of the euonymus snaking around a tree near the porch appeal to flickers in winter. Well-stocked feeders add to the avian attractions. The sound of falling water in a combination fountain/birdbath attracts migrant birds, such as orioles, scarlet tanagers, and many warblers, which normally do not frequent feeding stations.

At the back of the Sideli home a screened porch overlooks the water feature, the feeders, and the gardens. Field guides, binoculars, and a spiral notebook stand ready on a nearby table to make note of visiting birds. A baseball cap with the Baltimore Oriole logo might serve double duty as bird-watching headgear.

Elsewhere in the house, art and pottery collected on the couple's foreign travels decorate the walls, along with carvings of a pair of pileated woodpeckers by Randy and Elaine Fisher of Dennis, Massachusetts, and a pair of red-bellied woodpeckers, a flicker, and a kingfisher, all carved by Don McKinlay of Madison, Connecticut. A framed print of the passenger pigeon by Alexander Wilson, one of Vince's birding heroes, has a prominent place. (Wilson himself saw the pigeon in flocks numbering millions of birds before it went extinct from overhunting.)

Across from the bird carvings is a bookcase with the household's most treasured collection—the boxed, leatherbound journals in which Vince recorded the observations and illustrations of the couple's birding experience from 1978 into the late 1990s.

Vince gives the same care and attention to the birding journals—indeed, probably much more of it—that he gives to house and garden. He was inspired by John Burroughs's call for nature lovers to develop "the habit of keeping a journal of one's thoughts and days." The naturalist observed, "The pleasure and value of every walk or journey we take may be doubled to us by carefully noting down the impressions it makes upon us. There is hardly anything that does not become much more in the telling than in the thinking or in the feeling."

1. *Passenger Pigeon.* 2. *Blue-mountain Warbler.* 3. *Hemlock W.*

Long-tailed Sylph

OPPOSITE: The long-tailed sylph, a Peruvian hummingbird, was sighted on a trip to the pre-Columbian Inca site, Machu Picchu, in 2006. For male sylphs seeking to attract mates during breeding season, the longer the tail the better. ABOVE LEFT AND NEAR LEFT: Sideli fills notebooks with extensive observations on his birding adventures home and abroad, then transcribes them and finally transfers them, accompanied by his artwork, to leather-bound journals. ABOVE RIGHT: The rufous-sided towhee is Sideli's "spark bird"—the bird that sparked his interest in bird watching when he first sighted it in the spring of 1966 at a feeder near the cottage he and his wife, Carol, had rented in West Redding, Connecticut.

Accordingly, Vince began taking copious notes while watching birds from his home daily and during the couple's adventures on birding trips to Africa, Central America, Australia, and Southeast Asia. He transcribes his handwritten notes from each trip onto typed pages, adding sharply rendered illustrations of birds and other subjects encountered along the way. The self-taught artist has drawn more than four hundred birds for the journals. Each year of observations and paintings merits its own exquisitely bound leather covers.

"Over the years I've referred to various volumes to confirm the date of some important family event," he says. "I've also reread passages in order to relive a particularly pleasant experience or association."

Sometimes the observations are of the mundane variety. A spring entry from one journal begins:

> This morning as we finished our income tax form . . . we caught two
> gray squirrels . . . and relocated them.

In another entry, the couple come upon a Baltimore oriole lying stunned in the road. They retrieve the bird, take it home, and nurse it back to health. One fall day, Vince comes upon thousands of grackles feeding in a cornfield near his house. He reports the sighting in his journal, then observes that birds are often judged on a sliding scale. "Even songsters like bobolinks, beloved in the north," he notes, "flock in the thousands when they migrate south and are regarded by southerners as marauding hordes which do real damage to crops."

The trips to foreign locales naturally yield more colorful sightings than a neighborhood in suburban Connecticut. A 1992 trip to Costa Rica, led by ornithologist Noble Proctor, included this remarkable sighting:

> We were alerted to the approach of scarlet macaws by their raucous calls
> as they descended from the distant hills where they had spent the day
> feeding on fruit and nut trees. Mostly by twos, but sometimes in groups
> of as many as ten, the birds assembled in trees across the river, where
> they sat noisily for a while before breaking away for the flight across the
> river and into the Carara Reserve, where they spend the night. Noble
> had counted the birds as they crossed and the final tally was 148.

The map shows a journey through Kenya, with a legend reading:

...obi National Park 2 Lake Naivasha– Hell's Gate 3 Gilgil 4 Nanyuki
...lo 6 Samburu Game Reserve 7 Lake Baringo– Lake Bogoria 8 Eldoret
...ega Forest Reserve 10 Kisumu 11 Lake Nakuru 12 Masai-Mara Game Rese...
...vo National Park East 14 Mombasa 15 Shimba Hills Game Reserve

A 1994 trip through Kenya, also led by Professor Proctor, is illustrated with a map showing fifteen points of interest visited by the Sidelis and their birding colleagues, including Nairobi National Park and various game preserves. In their travels, the group crossed the equator several times. One afternoon at Lake Bogoria was particularly memorable:

Our first glimpse of the lake was from quite a distance, and it appeared as though the surface was covered with pink water lilies. It was only when we got much closer that we could make out the shapes of the lesser and greater flamingos, estimated to number one to two million.

Vince Sideli remains several years behind in his project to record his global birding life, but the backlog doesn't bother him. He has no set deadline, and indeed, his work is unfinished by its very nature. Like a Möbius strip, it goes on and on, giving pleasure along the way.

OPPOSITE: The drawing of the cardinal (above) was inspired by a sighting of twenty-two cardinals at one of Sideli's feeders, an unusually high number for a non-flocking species, yet "a lovely sight in the snow." Depicted in the journal for 1978 is Vince's favorite shorebird, a male ruddy turnstone in breeding plumage (below). ABOVE: An expedition to Nairobi National Park in July of 1994 reached its birding crescendo at Lake Bogoria with a sighting of more than a million flamingoes. FOLLOWING PAGES: Abundant flowering plants and vines, well-stocked feeders, and a good-sized water feature draw birds onto the Sidelis' property.

fpo #644

BUILD IT AND THEY WILL COME

Speaking to a group called the Mad Gardeners in Connecticut, National Audubon Society ornithologist Stephen Kress gave useful advice on improving the habitat for birds in one's own backyard. Kress, author of *The Audubon Society Guide to Attracting Birds*, cited examples from his own experience in buying a property in Ithaca, New York, where he teaches popular classes at the Cornell Laboratory of Ornithology.

"Like most suburban tracts, our land was not welcoming to birds," he said. "Manicured lawns treated with chemicals are actually sterile habitats not good for wildlife. We decided to cut back on our lawn and create a prairie instead. We mowed the remaining lawn less often, letting the grass grow to three or four inches. We nurtured an allée of sugar maples along the driveway to provide food, shelter, and singing perches and planted native shrubs and wildflowers for birds."

DR. KRESS PROVIDED THESE
ADDITIONAL TIPS

- Add a water feature to your yard; the sight and sound of moving water will attract birds that don't normally come to feeders.

- Create ground-level layers of brush at the edges of woodland where birds can seek refuge.

- Provide birds a small dust bath area composed of soil, wood ash, and pea gravel to help them rid their feathers of mites and lice.

- Plant native trees that bear fruit, berries, and other sources of protein for birds throughout the year, including oaks, dogwoods, hawthorns, magnolias, cherries, serviceberries, and shrubs such as viburnums, bayberry, and spice bush.

- Instead of removing dead trees, leave some of them for woodpeckers to use as drumming stations and for cavity nesters to use as nesting sites, and enhance the work of woodpeckers by drilling one-inch holes into the trees at an angle to give birds such as titmice and chickadees a starting point for carving out their nest cavities.

- Rake leaves under shrubs to create feeding areas for ground-feeders such as sparrows, thrashers, and towhees.

- Set out a shallow birdbath, elevated on a pedestal, for birds to drink from; scrub it clean and replace the water every few days.

- Allow a generous portion of your lawn to revert to field conditions with meadow plants and tall grasses that produce seeds for birds to eat. Cut down the field late in the year to encourage birds with declining populations, such as meadowlarks and bobolinks, to establish their ground nests in spring and summer.

- Outfit large glass windows in your house with mesh netting to prevent fatal collisions of bird on glass; an estimated one billion birds die from such crashes every year in the United States. (Experimental glass with embedded ultraviolet strips deter birds, which, unlike humans, can see UV, but the product is still in development.)

- Keep your cats inside the house. The cats will live longer, and so will your birds.

HOG ISLAND'S
"SOUNDS AND SWEET AIRS"

I WAS JUST NINE YEARS OLD WHEN I READ AN ACCOUNT BY ROGER TORY PETERSON ABOUT A MAGICAL PLACE CALLED AUDUBON CAMP," KENN KAUFMAN HAS WRITTEN, "A SPOT WHERE WARBLERS AND THRUSHES SANG FROM THE SPRUCES, WHERE EAGLES AND OSPREYS AND LOONS CRUISED BY OFFSHORE."

A boy growing up in Kansas can be forgiven for romanticizing a faraway island in Maine to which his hero introduced him, but Kaufman's descriptions hit the mark. Like the island in Shakespeare's *The Tempest,* Muscongus Bay's Hog Island "is full of noises, sounds, and sweet airs that give delight and hurt not." The three-hundred-acre enclave of pristine spruce and fir forest, a five-minute ride by lobster boat from the Maine coast, not far from Damariscotta, is a place that has been working its magic on birders and naturalists for seventy-five years.

In 1936, Peterson identified Hog Island as the ideal location for a summer camp to be set up by the National Audubon Society, for the purpose of training elementary and high school teachers in field science and the natural world. According to Peterson, "one youth leader could influence hundreds of individuals during the course of that person's career." Since then more than twenty-five thousand teachers have been exposed to the concept of ecology, with birds playing a central role in the curriculum.

Peterson served as the camp's main bird instructor that first summer of operation during six two-week sessions. His assistant was Allan D. Cruickshank, a charismatic Scot and a pioneer of bird photography. To this day,

Yellow-legs   Allan D. Cruickshank

PRECEDING PAGES: The noted field guide author Kenn Kaufman leads a group of teenagers onto Hog Island in Maine for a week of field identification, bird song recognition, and the chance to see first-hand the Audubon Society's seabird conservation efforts, including visits to the restored puffin colony on Eastern Egg Rock. OPPOSITE: The work of pioneering bird photographer Allan D. Cruickshank, who was an instructor at Hog Island for more than twenty years, beginning in 1936, is on display throughout the camp. ABOVE: A class on bird banding, a technique for taking a census of bird populations, provokes rapt attention among aspiring naturalists.

ABOVE: Even Hog Island's extracurricular puzzles have a pedagogical purpose. ABOVE RIGHT: Stephen Kress, director of National Audubon's Seabird Restoration Program, was Hog Island's camp director in 2010. He is shown with the carrying case he devised for transporting puffin chicks from Newfoundland to Muscongus Bay in 1973 in a successful effort to restore Maine's puffin population. OPPOSITE: Awaiting the next boat to the mainland, eighteen-year-old Jordan Budnik called her stay on Hog Island "the best week of my life."

Cruickshank's striking black-and-white studies of birds hang in the camp's dining room and dorm rooms. (*Life* magazine once ran a photo of "Cruicky" perched at the top of a hundred-foot tree, shooting close-ups of nesting ospreys with his cumbersome eight-by-ten-inch camera.)

In 2010, 166 participants from thirty-five states, many of them teenagers, spent a week visiting birding hotspots on the mainland and various islands, banding birds, and attending classes on seabird biology, conservation, and avian behaviors, organized by Stephen Kress, a former Hog Island director and founder of Audubon's acclaimed Project Puffin.

"It was the best week of my life," said Jordan Budnik, an eighteen-year-old participant from Atlanta, Georgia. She was particularly impressed with the classes given by Kenn Kaufman—who had come full circle from his boyhood fantasies about Hog Island.

"Once you spend a week on that island, it can be a life-changing experience," says Judy Braus, senior vice president for education of the National Audubon Society. "You interact with other participants in this ecologically diverse place; I've seen people come with one set of values and expectations and in one week have changed them."

One of the highlights for campers in 2010 was the boat ride to Eastern Egg Rock to witness firsthand a thriving colony of Atlantic puffins. By the 1970s, this species, which had been synonymous with the Maine coast, had vanished due to predation and habitat destruction. At that time, as a young researcher, Dr. Kress began transplanting puffin chicks annually from Canada to Maine,

ABOVE: Teaching materials in Hog Island's ornithology classes include images of species designed to foster identification of birds on the fly. OPPOSITE: Staffers dressed up as Hog Island's official mascot, the Atlantic puffin, bid farewell to departing students at week's end. FOLLOWING PAGES: Campers arrive on Hog Island at the early 1800s building called Queen Mary, originally a chandlery used to supply sea-going vessels with nautical gear and other commodities. Since 1936, when Roger

Many birders are addicted to making lists of birds they have seen, from backyard feeder lists to life lists, from Big Sit lists covering a single day to Big Year lists taking up an entire calendar year, from warblers to owls to shorebirds.

On at least one occasion, birders make lists not to celebrate their accomplishments but for the greater good, while participating in the Audubon Society's annual Christmas Bird Count. This census originated in 1900 and was the brainchild of Frank M. Chapman, ornithologist at the American Museum of Natural History in New York City and an early officer of the budding Audubon Society.

Chapman built on an earlier tradition known as the Christmas Side Hunt, in which participants chose sides and went afield with their guns; whoever brought in the biggest pile of feathered (and furry) quarry was declared the winner.

Conservation was in its beginning stages around the turn of the twentieth century, and like many scientists, Chapman was concerned about declining bird populations. He proposed a new holiday tradition that called for counting the birds during the holidays rather than shooting them. It would turn birders into "citizen scientists" and yield valuable data on the health and status of bird species across the country.

The tradition debuted with some twenty-seven bird watchers counting birds in twenty-five locations, mostly in or near urban areas of the Northeast, on Christmas Day, 1900. Since then, the count has grown into a national phenomenon with thousands of enthusiastic participants.

hoping they would return to their stateside location after spending their first two years of life at sea. Eight years passed before Dr. Kress beheld a puffin flying over Eastern Egg Rock with several fish in its bill. The "wildly joyous sighting" took place on the Fourth of July, 1981, and surpassed anything that year's fireworks could set off in the way of emotion. Puffin numbers have continued to increase at Eastern Egg Rock, with ninety-nine nests discovered by midsummer of 2010. Tern populations are also being nurtured on other Audubon-managed islands in the Gulf of Maine.

Along with Allan D. Cruickshank's vintage bird photos, poetry and verse hang in simple frames throughout the sleeping cottages and classrooms of the Hog Island Audubon Camp. One of the framed poems, by Rachel Field, a Maine islander and well-known children's book and adult fiction author in the 1930s, dwells on the transformative effects of island life, ending:

> *But once you've slept on an island,*
> *You'll never be quite the same.*

BIRDS ARE US

BILL THOMPSON III, THE EDITOR OF THE POPULAR BIMONTHLY *BIRD WATCHER'S DIGEST*, HAD A REALIZATION WHEN A NEIGHBOR'S WOODS CAUGHT FIRE AND HE CLIMBED ONTO HIS OWN ROOF TO SEE THE EXTENT OF THE BLAZE.

"I saw what a great view I had of the surrounding countryside," he recalls, "and then and there I decided to build a tower next to the house from which my wife and I could enjoy the view and, of course, see birds."

The top of the tower, reached by staircase and ladder, stands forty-two feet above ground level, and seldom does a day pass without Bill or his wife, Julie Zickefoose, another renowned birder, ascending it with binoculars in hand. From this vantage point, the couple's eighty-acre farm, called Indigo Hill, in the Appalachian foothills of Ohio spreads below them like a living tapestry. Its orchards, pastures, and woodlands offer glimpses of cardinals and meadowlarks, bobolinks and hawks, bluebirds and hummingbirds, not to mention species like bobcats, foxes, and a Boston terrier named Chet Baker.

"The tower has proven to be a great joy for us," says Julie. "It's like being on a boat at sea."

Bill became interested in bird watching at the age of eight, when he saw a snowy owl in the front yard of his family's home in Pella, Iowa. Julie was seven and growing up in Richmond, Virginia, when she became captivated by a blue-winged warbler. She not only watched birds at an early age, she painted them. "My parents gave me a book with the work of Louis Agassiz Fuertes in it," she recalls. "There were other bird painters represented in the book, but I admired Fuertes because I saw a truth there that made me think he'd been looking right at the bird as he painted."

Bill majored in environmental studies and journalism at Western College of Miami University in Oxford, Ohio, then worked as an account executive for the advertising firm Ogilvy & Mather in New York. Julie studied biological anthropology at Harvard before taking a job with The Nature Conservancy in Connecticut. Their paths crossed at *Bird Watcher's Digest* in 1990. The magazine has been the pivotal venue for Julie's work since she wrote her first piece for it in 1986, and her bird paintings have appeared on more than twenty covers.

Thompson is another birder whose life and career were touched by Roger Tory Peterson. *Bird Watcher's Digest* was launched by Bill's parents, Bill Thompson Jr. and Elsa Thompson, from their Marietta, Ohio, family room in 1978. The senior Thompson decided to send a copy of the first issue to Peterson, inviting him to comment on the new publication. When Peterson responded with a long critique, focused but friendly, of the magazine's contents, Bill's parents jumped for joy. As icing on the cake, Peterson also enclosed a check for a subscription.

Ten years later, Bill accompanied his father to Hawk Mountain, a bird observatory in Kempton, Pennsylvania, for a gathering of birders celebrating the sanctuary's sixtieth anniversary. Peterson was to be the keynote speaker. By now Bill was twenty-six and an associate editor of *Bird Watcher's Digest*.

At a book signing following Peterson's talk, Bill Jr. introduced his son to Roger after waiting in line for some time. Roger stood up from the table where he was signing his books, shook the younger Thompson's hand, and then, to Bill III's surprise, asked him to follow the famous birder outside the tent where the book signing was taking place.

"You've got young ears and I don't," Peterson explained when they'd left the tent. "Can you tell me what you think of the sounds those katydids are making? They sound quite different from our katydids in Connecticut."

"I didn't know what to think," Thompson recalls. "I knew what a katydid sounded like, but I had never thought about regional differences in their calls."

"There, did you hear that one?" he exclaimed. "Quite a bit thinner and higher than ours in Connecticut."

A 14-day old chimney swift,
last to leave the nest.
Its eyes have just
opened. Now it will
crowd, climb and
exercise its wings
for another 14
days, until it's
ready to leave
the chimney
for good.

The little
hammock of a nest
is shiny, lacquered with
the adults' saliva— all that
holds it together.

"I nodded my assent," Thompson relates, "and we stood a few minutes more—the world's most accomplished field guide author and an awestruck young man, listening to insect calls in the dark while hundreds of adoring fans waited a few dozen feet away. Those minutes alone with him are something I will always cherish."

Two years after his katydid summit meeting with Peterson, Bill met Julie, and soon after they married and moved to the farm. Today, their daughter, Phoebe, and son, Liam, round out the family, along with Charlie, a twenty-one-year-old chestnut-fronted macaw who hangs around Julie's studio. The studio doubles as an infirmary for orphaned and injured birds and other small animals. Accounts of Julie's rescues often figure in her blog and her commentaries for National Public Radio. "I have a life bite list," she says, "of animals who've bitten me, mostly in captivity."

Bill's blog, which attracts more than a thousand daily readers from around the world, posts both lighthearted and thoughtful reports on bird happenings at Indigo Hill, such as a pair of pileated woodpeckers building their nest in a dead tree. The couple travel widely, leading birders on field trips and giving programs at many of the more than four hundred bird festivals organized every year across the country.

Thompson has watched birds in twenty-five countries and forty-eight states, but the farm remains his favorite place for birding. Every fall, he and Julie invite friends and neighbors to the farm to take part in a sedentary form of bird watching called the Big Sit. A member of the New Haven Bird Club in Connecticut came up with the idea years ago, as a way of tuning into the fall migration of birds, and it has since grown into a one-day birdathon popular throughout the United States and abroad. Groups of birders are encouraged to locate a good birding spot in their area, sit in a circle for twenty-four hours (alternating shifts is within the rules), and count the birds that come within their ken. In many instances, the Big Sit results in sightings of fifty or more species.

"We use our tower for the Big Sit," says Bill. "With friends we just sit there for hours at a time, letting the birds come to us, and then we have a potluck supper."

According to Thompson, birding has grown by leaps and bounds since the founding of his magazine. "Back in the 1970s and '80s, it was traumatic being a bird watcher because of the Miss Jane Hathaway caricature," he recalls. (Miss Jane, a character in the TV show *The Beverly Hillbillies,* was depicted as a love-starved spinster who wore a pith helmet on her bird watching forays.) "Then a Ross's gull from the Arctic showed up in Newburyport in 1978 and stayed for

OPPOSITE: Nestling eastern bluebirds in the birdhouse at the end of the driveway at Indigo Hill are found to be in good condition by Bill and Julie. A gentle hands-on intrusion is not harmful to the young birds, but the human activity is closely monitored from a nearby location by one or both parent birds.

several weeks. Birders flocked to Massachusetts by the thousands just to see this one bird, and I thought, 'My God, I'm not alone!'"

Thompson's enthusiasm for birds and birding runs deep and is infectious. "The easiest way to get into the natural world is through birds," he observes. "They're everywhere and they're so noticeable." Then he ticks off the unique combination of features found in the bird species: "They are beautiful. They sing amazing songs. They perform weird and amazing behaviors, from migrations to courtship displays. And last but not least, they fly!"

FOLLOWING PAGE: Not surprisingly a bookcase in the Thompson/Zickefoose household is chock-full of books.

WHAT'S IN BILL'S BIRD BAG?

Bill Thompson doesn't carry all this gear with him on every birding trip, but this is the extensive equipment supply closet he draws from when he makes his picks for any trek. The information appears on billofthebirds.blogspot and is updated there from time to time, along with vivid accounts of Thompson's most recent birding travels and updates on the bird life on his farm at Indigo Hill.

BINOCULARS: Zeiss Victory FL 8×42, Swarovski EL 10×42

SCOPE: Swarovski ATS 65mm with 20–60× zoom eyepiece

TRIPOD: Bogen Manfrotto 055CX3 carbon fiber tripod, with Bogen 3130 Micro-fluid style pan head

CARRIERS: Mountainsmith Tour recycled materials lumbar pack; Pajaro Grande field guide pack; LowePro Toploader 75W camera bag with harness belt

CLOTHING: *Outerwear:* Arc'Teryx waterproof shell; Mountain Hardwear breathable rain jacket; Helly Hansen insulate rain jacket. *Hat:* Dorfman Pacific field hat. *Shoes:* Keen Newports; Arroyos; and Arubas. *Boots:* Merrell Moab Ventilator Mid; Muck Boots Wetland insulated rubber boots

FIELD GUIDES: *Peterson Field Guide to Birds of North America* (Houghton Mifflin, 2008); *The Sibley Guide to Birds* (Knopf, 2000); *The Young Birder's Guide to Birds of Eastern North America* (Houghton Mifflin, 2008); Kaufman Field Guides (Birds, Mammals, Butterflies, Insects) (Houghton Mifflin)

COMPUTER: Apple MacBook Pro laptop

SOUND: Apple 8G iPhone with iBird app; Apple 4G iPod Nano with birdJam

software; Creative TravelSound i80 speaker MF5110; Motorola T6500 walkie-talkies

SIGHT: Petzl Tikka headlamp; RadioShack green laser pointer, model 63-132

IMAGING: Canon EOS 30D Digital SLR camera with 300mm fixed IS lens (for bird photography); Canon EOS Digital Rebel XSi camera with 18–55mm lens (for landscape photography); Canon PowerShot A590IS 8MP digital camera (for digiscoping) with Swarovski digiscoping adapter and Canon LA-DC52F conversion lens adapter

TOP AND RIGHT: From their forty-two-foot tower, Julie and Bill keep track of both native birds and migrants moving through the area in the spring and fall.
ABOVE: *Bird Watcher's Digest,* a bimonthly magazine started by the Thompson family in Marietta, Ohio, in 1978 and now edited by Bill Thompson III features original artwork on its covers, including twenty of Julie's paintings.

WHAT'S IN JULIE'S SUET?

This recipe is popular with jays, titmice, nuthatches, chickadees, woodpeckers, sparrows, towhees, cardinals, bluebirds, mockingbirds, thrashers, warblers, and, of course, our avaricious starlings. It is reprinted with permission from Julie Zickefoose's blog, juliezickefoose. blogspot.com.

Please feed responsibly! Avoid feeding lard-based foods to birds during the warm spring and summer months, when they can find ample and natural sources of nourishment themselves. Birds that gorge on suet and other lard-based recipes run the risk of developing gout. Suet is best served during the winter months, and especially during harsh weather conditions.

TO MAKE JULIE'S SUET
Melt in the microwave and stir together:
    1 cup peanut butter
    1 cup lard
    In a large mixing bowl, combine:
    2 cups chick starter (unmedicated,
       available at any feed store)
    2 cups quick oats
    1 cup yellow cornmeal
    1 cup flour

Add the melted lard/peanut butter mixture to the combined dry ingredients and mix well.

PART II

BIRD
HOUSES

Observe the singular vision of passionate birders in their homes, studios, and getaways
as they shape and color these haunts with such conviction that you can almost hear
the song of the warbler, the quack of the duck, the screech of the owl. Here the call of
the wild is beautiful and true.

AUDUBON MAN

I T IS PROBABLY TYPICAL THAT WHEN DONAL C. O'BRIEN JR. RECEIVED THE PRESTIGIOUS AUDUBON MEDAL IN SEPTEMBER OF 2010, HE SPENT MOST OF HIS ACCEPTANCE SPEECH CREDITING OTHER PEOPLE FOR THEIR EFFORTS ON BEHALF OF BIRDS AND CONSERVATION. THE HONOR PLACED HIM IN GOOD COMPANY. PREVIOUS MEDAL WINNERS INCLUDE WILLIAM O. DOUGLAS, RACHEL CARSON, STEWART UDALL, LAURANCE S. ROCKEFELLER, ALDO LEOPOLD, ROBERT REDFORD, AND JIMMY CARTER.

As a board member of the Audubon Society for twenty-five years and its chair for fifteen, O'Brien's deeds on behalf of conservation are many, but he is most proud of implementing a program to designate Important Bird Areas, or IBAs, in North America as a way of protecting and preserving the flyways of migratory birds and "to link the sites that birds need to breed, winter, rest, and refuel during spring and fall migrations."

Some twenty-five hundred IBAs have been identified by Audubon to date, with the goal of doubling that number in the near future. The challenge is that only a third of the areas are currently protected, while a third are facing threats, and another third are critically endangered.

The 1740 Connecticut house where Donal lives with his wife, Katie, is a kind of IBA itself, with the holdings of a discriminating small wildlife museum and the lived-in character of a home with black Labs and English setters underfoot. A broad hall adjacent to the kitchen is lined with original Audubon prints depicting a pair of snowy owls, a great blue heron, a pair of Icelandic falcons in flight, an osprey, two canvasback ducks, and a pair of long-billed curlews.

PRECEDING PAGES: A collection of original Audubon prints in the entry hall makes a stunning first impression on visitors to the Connecticut home of Donal O'Brien, a staunch conservationist who served on the board of National Audubon for twenty-five years. OPPOSITE: The bedroom is a showcase for Donal O'Brien's vast collection of carved and painted shorebirds and duck decoys. Above *November*, an oil painting by Ogden Pleissner, is a collection of pie crimpers made of scrimshaw by mariners during idle time on long voyages in whaling ships.

The hall spills into a living room filled with hundreds of duck and goose decoys from Connecticut, Cape Cod, Maine, Long Island, and Chesapeake Bay, executed by such carvers of high repute as Albert Laing, "the Michelangelo of decoy makers," according to Donal; Shang Wheeler; Elmer Crowell; Lem Ward; and Donal O'Brien himself (although he would characterize his many prize-winning creations as the work of an amateur). Over the mantel, a large water-color by Aiden Lassell Ripley shows a flock of ruffed grouse feeding on apples among the bare branches of a tree. Wing shooting and angling scenes by renowned sporting artist Ogden Pleissner, whom Donal knew as a friend, animate other walls.

"Birds are my passion, but I care about everything from blue claw crabs to African elephants, and I want to protect them all," says O'Brien, a retired Wall Street law firm partner who represented the interests of the Rockefeller family as well as other clients. When he and Katie traveled to Mexico for their first Audubon board meeting in 1976, "we were taken out on a bird walk," he recalls, "and we saw this vermilion flycatcher sitting on a thistle. It was heartbreaking in its beauty, and we've been birding every since."

Growing up, ducks were Donal's bird of choice. "I just loved the way they flew, the way they looked, the different habits they exhibited," he says. "I've been watching them for so long I can identify every species of duck in North America from a half mile away, just by looking at the way they move through the air."

In his prime, O'Brien and other hardy hunters indulged in the risky business of shooting ducks from the icy seawalls off Long Island Sound on weekends in the depth of winter. Frostbite and worse could result from rowing four miles over open water with shotgun, Labrador retriever, and a rig of decoys, but each time he went out, the experience left him revitalized for tackling professional life on Monday mornings. Hunting for ruffed grouse and woodcock and

fly fishing, which he learned from the master, Lee Wulff, also have figured prominently on his sporting calendar over the years.

Journals documenting O'Brien's sporting trips and birding expeditions, along with numerous books on decoys and decoy carving, form an integral part of an extensive library that claims bookshelf space wherever it can, amid figures of shorebirds, stoneware crocks, Nantucket baskets, and folk art pieces, such as the man imagined as a crow, that make even the most sober visitors nod and smile.

Beneath a broad window in Donal's sunlit office, a herd of elephants, cast in bronze in a variety of naturalistic poses, appear to be moving single file across their own version of the Serengeti Plain. Paperwork seems to have the upper hand on O'Brien's outsized desk. Retired in name alone, he remains involved in a host of conservation groups, including National Audubon, the Atlantic Salmon Federation, BirdLife International, and The Nature Conservancy. "My years as a conservationist have been the driving force in my not-for-profit life," he observes. In his home state of Connecticut he has served on the State Board of Fisheries and Game and on the Council of Environmental Quality under three governors over a thirty-year period.

But Donal O'Brien is not just shuffling papers in his office. He is often on the phone, lighting fires for important causes. Like two of his personal heroes, John James Audubon and Theodore Roosevelt, he combines the vision of the artist with the courage of the crusader. "You can't do conservation without advocacy and wise public policy," he says, echoing the sentiments of those conservation pioneers. "If we don't advocate for birds and achieve conservation, we will have failed to realize our mission."

AVIAN TAJ MAHAL

THE NAME "BULL RUN FARM" CONJURES UP THE IMAGE OF A TEXAS-STYLE CATTLE SPREAD, BUT THE BUCOLIC COUNTRY PROPERTY OF DONNA AND PATRICK ANNUNZIATA, TUCKED INTO THE BERKSHIRE HILLS OF SOUTHWESTERN MASSACHUSETTS, IS AS QUIETLY ELEGANT AS ITS DOVECOTE OF SNOW-WHITE PIGEONS.

Two dozen Saudi Arabian frillback pigeons live large in a round stone house with grilled windows and a majestic mahogany finial at the apex of its sloping roof. Donna lets the birds out of their well-furnished coop every day for the chance to exercise their wings and to bathe in an old stone trough. "They're not great fliers," she says, "so they never venture far from home."

The hexagonal dovecote anchors a garden, fifty by eighty feet, with three stone walls and a fourth wall, facing the main house, made of wooden posts, chicken wire, and an arched gate with a honeycomb lattice. Designed by Nancy McCabe, the garden was inspired by the art and architecture of India's Mughal Empire, a style that would not seem at first glance like an easy fit for its tradition-bound New England location.

"We're very adventurous people," says Donna, who founded the Donna Morgan fashion label and who, with her husband, Patrick, a fabric importer, embraced Nancy's unique concept for their garden. "We wanted something whimsical, a garden folly, really. So we didn't have to think too long once we

saw her plans," Donna continues. "Even during construction we knew it was going to work beautifully on our property, because the house is Federal and everything else is really plain. The asymmetrical garden plan, the neutral colors of the stone walls, and the weathered mahogany blend wonderfully with the house."

Nancy McCabe herself has been in and out of all sorts of gardens since she was a child. Her father, an entomologist with the U.S. Department of Agriculture, had a great love of the land and birds. "Everything revolved around nature for us," says Nancy. "It's just how we lived." Today, her two brothers are renowned ornithologists: Frank Rohwer, a professor at Louisiana State University, whose area of expertise is waterfowl, and Sievert Rohwer, a professor at the University of Washington, curator of birds at the Burke Museum in Seattle and recipient of the Elliott Coues Lifetime Achievement Award for extraordinary contributions to ornithological research.

Dovecotes have long played a role in gardening history, according to McCabe. They were a symbol of status and power in the Middle Ages, and of practicality. Pigeons and doves were an important food source, providing their owner's household with meat and eggs, not to mention excellent manure for fertilizing gardens.

The Annunziatas' own garden rewards them with the beauty of flowers blooming in sequence throughout the growing season, including baptisia, phlox, delphinium, salvia, peonies, geraniums, and Siberian iris, and food for the table in the form of rhubarb, Swiss chard, cabbage, and fennel. A weeping pear medlar, apple trees espaliered on the south-facing stone wall, and raspberry canes provide fresh fruit.

For Donna Annunziata, the dovecote garden is not just a source of provisions and a thing of beauty. It is also a good excuse to get her hands dirty. "If I just sat out there with a glass of wine in the evening, admiring the flowers and the birds, I would feel the garden didn't belong to me," she says. "The most important thing to me is rolling up my sleeves and working in the trenches."

PRECEDING PAGES: A walled garden designed by Nancy McCabe is anchored by an Anglo-Indian aviary and planted with perennial flowers that thrive in the climate of western Massachusetts. ABOVE AND OPPOSITE: A flock of Saudi Arabian frillback pigeons live a pampered existence in their custom-designed quarters. Released once a day, the birds enjoy their freedom, often bathing in a water trough provided for them, but never stray far from the garden. FOLLOWING PAGES: Constructed of stone and mahogany, the walls and gates surrounding the fifty-by-eighty-foot garden incorporate arches and hexagonals associated with Mughal Empire design.

NESTING INSTINCTS

FROM THE OUTSIDE, THE CIRCA-1900 HOUSE SECRETED AMONG SHRUBS AND GARDENS IN THE HEIGHTS, ONE OF THE OLDEST NEIGHBORHOODS IN HOUSTON, TEXAS, LOOKS LIKE A QUIET RETREAT FROM THE CLAMOR OF URBAN LIFE. INSIDE, THE HOUSE OF ARTISTS LISA LUDWIG AND JOSEPH HAVEL IS ANYTHING BUT SEDATE.

The residence is furnished with an eclectic mix of furnishings and art, including one of Lisa's bronze bird's nest sculptures, so realistic one expects to see a live bird alight on it at any moment. And there's a remote chance one will, specifically Lisa's pet African gray parrot, Hannah.

Hannah has free reign in the house, but usually hangs out in the living room, near the aviary Lisa has built to accommodate the injured and orphaned birds she takes in and tends to until they can be safely released. The bird colony included a group of diamond doves, assorted finches, a white dove named Milagro, and an Inca dove that Lisa found at the ranch where she keeps and rides her horse.

The parrot can imitate the calls of all the birds in the aviary, as well as Lisa's cats. "She uses my voice to talk to Joe and vice versa," says Lisa. "Sometimes she imitates my laugh while I'm talking on the phone, so that it sounds like I'm calling from an asylum. She likes to ride in the car and occasionally perches on the steering wheel, squealing *wheeee* with every turn. But we have curtailed that very dangerous amusement."

PRECEDING PAGES: A small aviary adjoining the kitchen was built to accommodate injured and orphaned birds, mostly doves and finches, which Lisa Ludwig nurses back to health so they can be released. ABOVE: In her studio, Lisa begins the deconstruction of a bird's nest, in preparation for casting it in bronze. OPPOSITE: Back from the foundry, the finished product is a graceful representation of one of nature's marvels.

Ever since childhood visits to her Aunt Bertie, who had a parrot named Polly living at home with her in Philadelphia, Lisa had wanted a parrot of her own. After moving to Houston, she stopped by a pet shop, "not parrot-shopping, but just to browse," she recalls, and saw a parrot named Stormy. "Stormy looked into my eyes and then flipped over backward and hung by one foot and said, 'Credit card.' It was a sign," Lisa laughs, "and sure enough, when I returned home that day, there was a message from the Moody Gallery, where my work was represented, that they had sold a piece of mine."

Lisa immediately got back in her car, drove to the pet shop, and "sprung" Stormy. But when she brought the bird to her veterinarian, DNA testing revealed that the parrot was female, not male as had been assumed, "and soon after, Stormy became Hannah."

Lisa's studio, visible from her living room, is a converted greenhouse. She creates her sculptures by beginning with real nests that she finds at the horse ranch. "I see a lot more when I am riding my horse than I do on foot," she says. "I prefer blue jay, dove, and mockingbird nests to work with because they are fittingly 'sticky.'" Each nest is surgically deconstructed to the point where it retains its structure as a nest, but is sufficiently reduced in "twigginess" to lend itself to being cast in bronze at the foundry.

"There," Lisa explains, "it is encased in a system of wax sprues—a vascular system that will allow the hot metal to reach each and every twig." The piece is covered with a ceramic shell, and then the wax and nest are burned out of the shell. The bronze is poured into the shell, and when it cools, the shell is broken away. "There is lots of meticulous sandblasting and sometimes soldering to be done," says Lisa. "Then I tweak the pieces and decide how they are going to be attached to the wall or stand independently."

Unlike Lisa's bronze creations, Hannah the parrot sometimes doesn't stay where installed. One particular escape remains fresh in Lisa's memory.

"She was perched on Joe's shoulder one evening when, without thinking, Joe stepped from the house into the backyard," Lisa relates. "The parrot immediately took wing and flew away. We spent a horrible night searching for her and putting up fliers."

The following morning, they spotted Hannah perched about forty feet up in a tree in the parking lot of a bank two blocks away from their house. "If the trees had been in leaf, we would not have seen her," Lisa says. "We called the fire department for help, but they weren't interested. Then I called the service that trims our trees. The dispatcher said he could send a cherry picker to us, but he estimated the cost would be several hundred dollars. Of course I agreed." (It turned out that the dispatcher had a parrot, too, and never did send a bill.)

The cherry picker arrived and parked at the base of the tree. Against regulation, the foreman allowed Joe to go up in the bucket with Hannah's carrier. He was able to grab the parrot and pop her into the carrier.

"Hannah, Joe, and I returned home exhausted but happy," Lisa says, "and we all shared a plate of scrambled eggs."

OPPOSITE: A nest given to Lisa by an artist friend in Miami sits jauntily above the work of a society portrait painter that came down through Lisa's family on her father's side. Beneath, the work of another friend, Minnesota potter Warner MacKenzie, has a place of honor. ABOVE: The house where two artists live reflects the eclectic taste of the owners, mixing the old, the new, and the unexpected. The cherry wood cabinet of the eighteenth-century grandfather's clock was made in Philadelphia. Lisa's parrot, Hannah, has the run of the house but is usually perched in or near her cage.

BIRDS IN THE GALLERY

The saying "A little bird told me so," dates from ancient times when birds were regarded as harbingers of things to come. Betty Moody of Houston, Texas, still believes that is so. "Birds alert me to what's going on in the natural world," she says. "I know it's January in Texas Hill Country when the flocks of robins, cedar waxwings, and bluebirds strip the yaupon bushes clean of their ripe red berries. If the birds are late or don't ever arrive, then I know something's wrong."

Since 1975, Betty's much esteemed Moody Gallery has been a harbinger of things to come in contemporary arts. "Our emphasis has always been on artists living and working in Texas," she explains, "as well as artists who have had a strong connection to Texas."

Birds figure prominently in the works of some of the artists Betty represents. "The symbolic nature of birds has long influenced artists," she says. "They respond to their beauty, their amazing

flight capabilities, and their ability to survive not just their natural environments but the obstacles that humans have put in their way."

Betty draws on work in the gallery to illustrate her points: the lifelike cast bronze nest sculptures of Lisa Ludwig (preceding pages); the aerodynamic drawing of a bird in flight by Bill Steffy; and the burn drawings by Helen Altman, who singes wet paper with a propane torch. "Up close, the bird form looks

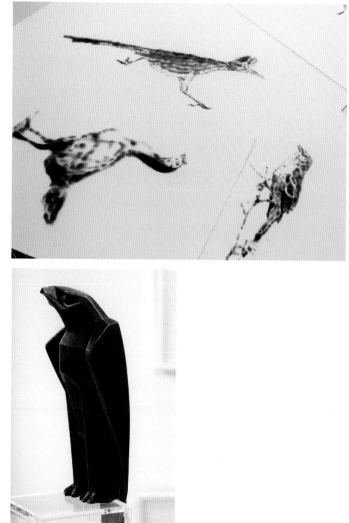

blurry, but when you step back, it comes into sharp focus," notes Betty. She holds up a raven study by Luis Jiménez taken from life. "Luis had a deep connection to birds," Betty observes. "He and his children would go to the zoo frequently, and he would sketch birds and other animals. He had pet ravens when he lived in Hondo, New Mexico. People would bring him injured birds, and he would nurse them until they were able to fly."

Depictions of birds can evoke a wide range of emotions. Photographers Ed Hill and Suzanne Bloom see conflict between our contemporary civilization and the natural world, "one in which nature is usually on the losing side," says Betty. But other artists find humor in their subjects, such as Jim Love, "who created a whole genus of droll bird sculptures made from 'found' scraps of steel and other materials."

Artistic interpretations of birds, Betty Moody concludes, "are as diverse as the birds themselves."

OPPOSITE: Artists and their works, clockwise from top left: *The Hummingbird's Equation*, ink and graphite by James Drake; Betty Moody with *Exotic Birds*, cut paper by Al Souza; *Chula*, lithograph by Luis Jimenez. **ABOVE:** Clockwise from left: *Scoop-Tailed Chef*, steel, cast iron, and brass by Jim Love; torch drawing on paper of roadrunners and mockingbird by Helen Altman; and *Bird*, cast bronze by Bill Steffy.

A BIRDER'S TREASURE ISLAND

WITH THEIR POWERFUL BINOCULARS AND SPOTTING SCOPES, SOLITARY BIRDERS IN REMOTE LOCATIONS ARE SOMETIMES SUSPECTED OF BEING CIA OPERATIVES. CLOSER TO HOME, THEY RISK THE INDIGNITY OF BEING TAKEN FOR PEEPING TOMS. THAT'S WHY THE HIGH ISLAND BIRD SANCTUARIES NEAR GALVESTON, TEXAS, ISSUE AN EXPLICIT WARNING TO THEIR PATRONS.

"Birds can be found anywhere on High Island, including our neighbors' yards," says the visitor's guide published by the Houston Audubon Society, which manages the four sanctuaries within walking distance of each other. "Please do not enter their yards, and be careful where you aim your binoculars, as some local residents get the idea that birders are looking in their windows and invading their privacy."

High Island's 255 acres of woods, coastal prairie, and wetlands are a magnet for birders from around the world in the spring and fall, the seasons of year when the many bird species classified as neotropical migrants travel between their winter grounds in Central and South America and their spring nesting locations in North America.

"The birds first push north to the Yucatán Peninsula and the adjacent Mexican coast," explains High Island sanctuaries manager Winnie Burkett. "Then, in early March, the migrants head north across the Gulf of Mexico," a voyage of 650 miles, which takes an average of eighteen hours in good weather. If wind and rain hamper their travel, they reach the Texas coast even more sorely in need of the food and rest that only a good-quality habitat such as High Island can offer. "That's when we get a lot of tired birds," says Winnie, "but we treasure the experience."

Birders adding species to their life lists are especially keen on High Island because on an average day, during the key seasons, more neotropical migrants are identified in its relatively tiny preserves than can be found in several thousand acres of the prime Appalachian forests where they make their homes and raise their young in the summer. Boardwalks and viewing platforms facilitate seeing the

birds, which feed on insects and berries before continuing their journey. Their presence on the Texas coastline is fleeting. "Depending on how tired they are," says Winnie, "they may not even stay the night."

High Island is located atop a salt dome, a common geological feature in Texas. In an earlier era, salt domes drew wildcatters like flies to honey, once it became known that enormous underground pools of oil were often found near them. Indeed, oil, natural gas, and sulfur have all been extracted from the sediments surrounding the dome at High Island.

A pond that was dug for a sulfur extraction plant in the 1950s enabled the creation of Heron Island, the sanctuary's most dazzling attraction, which hosts as many as nine thousand birds at one time. "The dirt dug out to create the pond was dumped in the middle. It makes a perfect retreat for nesting species like roseate spoonbills and snowy egrets," says Winnie. "Predators such as coyotes and raccoons can't get to the nests because there are alligators in the waters surrounding the island."

Bleacher seats, of the sort commonly seen greenside at golf tournaments, have been erected at the Boy Scout Woods Sanctuary, a short walk from Heron Island. A pipe dripping a constant flow of water had been established in a copse

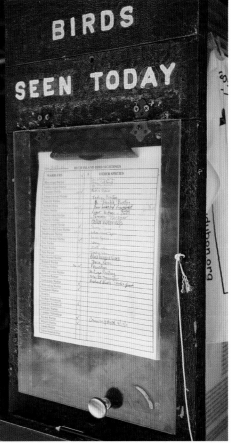

PRECEDING PAGES: A roseate spoonbill flies in some nesting material at the High Island Bird Sanctuaries in Texas. OPPOSITE, ABOVE: Bleachers were installed to provide birders with a place to sit down and enjoy fairly close and open views of songbirds coming to a water drip to drink and bathe. OPPOSITE, BELOW: Adam Wood, as field trip coordinator for the Houston Audubon Society, leads groups to the many rich birding locales that Texas offers. LEFT AND ABOVE: Birders of all ages follow the action during the spring migration of birds on the Gulf Coast, with sightings dutifully recorded at a central location in the sanctuary. FOLLOWING PAGES: Spoonbills and snowy egrets, among other waterbirds, build their nests and raise their chicks on an island made safe from bird and egg predators by the presence of alligators in the surrounding waters.

of woods near the entrance to the sanctuary. This water source attracted many birds and, soon, crowds of bird watchers ensconced in lawn chairs. "Things got so tight we decided to raise money to build a grandstand," says Winnie. "When the birding is good, the stands are always full."

According to legend, Jean Lafitte and his crew threw raucous parties in the grove of oak trees that covered the island when pirates cruised the coast in the early 1800s, looking for ships to plunder. Numerous searches for the treasure rumored to be buried here by Lafitte's confederates have come up empty. The only treasure High Island can rightfully claim is its birds, and for bird watchers, that is a small fortune indeed.

BIRDER'S CODE
OF CONDUCT

The Houston Audubon Society has developed simple guidelines for how human visitors to its bird sanctuaries should conduct themselves in order to minimize stress on the birds—and fellow birders. Their advice could be beneficial to bird watchers in any nature preserve.

- No dogs.
- No weapons.
- No cell phones.
- No smoking.
- No bird calls or laser beams.
- Stay on trails and boardwalks.
- Beware of mosquitoes, venomous snakes, poison ivy, and other dangers of the wild.
- Curb your enthusiasm—loud conversations distress birds and birders alike.

A DAY AT THE MUSEUM

KRISTOF ZYSKOWSKI, MANAGER OF THE VERTEBRATE COLLECTION AT YALE'S PEABODY MUSEUM OF NATURAL HISTORY, STARTED BIRDING BEFORE HE KNEW IT. AT THE AGE OF FOUR, GROWING UP IN SEJNY, A SMALL TOWN NEAR THE LITHUANIAN BORDER IN NORTHEASTERN POLAND, THE LAD BECAME FIXATED ON A NEST OF HOUSE MARTINS THAT THE FAMILY WOULD PASS ON THE WAY TO WEEKEND MATINEES AT THE LOCAL CINEMA.

"I have no personal recollection of it at all," he says, "but my parents assure me that every time we walked by the nest, I insisted on stopping until I got to see one of the parent birds come to the nest with food for their young." He adds, "Apparently we were late for the movies on more than one occasion."

By first grade, Kristof was keeping a nature journal, logging the names of birds as they arrived in Sejny in the spring, for example. At first snow in the winter, his father, an avid hunter and fisher, would take Kristof and his brother, Jerzy, into the woods, show them animal tracks, and generally inspire them with the wonders of the natural world. He brought home guide books for them and other treatises on natural science, and regularly quizzed the boys to be sure they understood what they were reading.

PRECEDING PAGES: The impressive forms of the griffon vulture and great bustard provide a striking counterpoint to Yale's ultramodern facility, opened in 2001, for storing its vast collection of birds, nests, and eggs. ABOVE: Vestiges of extinct bird species are found in the skeleton of the great auk, the last flightless bird of the northern hemisphere, and in study skins of the passenger pigeon and Carolina parakeet. ABOVE RIGHT: Kristof Zyskowski is Yale's manager of vertebrate collections. OPPOSITE: Eggs of the thick-billed murre are unique in the sense that no two patterns on the eggs produced by this species are alike, a fact which helps each mother bird to recognize her own egg in the nesting colony. FOLLOWING PAGES: A grouping of taxidermy includes the familiar barnyard bird, the more exotic hornbill, the California condor, and a large flightless bird, the cassowary of New Guinea and Australia.

Three decades later, Zyskowski's desire to precisely understand the natural world, in particular the world of birds, has grown exponentially. In 2000, he accepted his present appointment at Yale, following the completion of his dissertation at the University of Kansas. While studying the nest architecture of South American ovenbirds for his PhD, he dispelled the myth that birds can alter nesting behaviors, which are in fact largely dictated by genetics. In other words, his thesis argued, if a species traditionally lines its nest with bamboo leaves, it's not going to change to twigs anytime soon.

Yale's house of avian science contains 140,000 bird specimens, or "study skins," representing 7,000 species. That equates to about seventy percent of the world's bird species and includes all but two families. A year after coming to New Haven, Kristof faced his first big job challenge: transferring the entire collection to the university's newly built Environmental Science Center, located around the corner from the Peabody Museum. The all-white, high-tech, temperature-controlled storage facility conveys the pristine efficiency of a Martha Stewart test kitchen.

"Moving everything was a chance to get hands-on knowledge of the entire collection," he says, "and at the same time, to reorganize the collection to reflect current knowledge of interrelationships among species." Historically, for example, grebes and loons were considered sister water birds, and flamingos were thought to be related to storks and herons. More recently, however, the work of molecular biologists has shown that these similarities are likely due to convergence (i.e., adaptations to similar environments) instead, and that, in

ABOVE: Yale's collection of study skins represents seven thousand species, including species of eubucco barbets, neotropical birds from the highland forests of Central and South America. The brilliant colors in certain birds are not susceptible to fading because the colors are produced by feather structure, not pigment. OPPOSITE, ABOVE: The Andean cock-of-the-rock is noted for its beautiful crest, tail feathers, and vivid coloration. Scientists are the primary users of Yale's avian collection, but wildlife artists interested in creating accurate portrayals of birds are also granted access. OPPOSITE, BELOW: The loosely constructed nest of the South American pale-vented pigeon usually contains two eggs in breeding season.

fact, grebes are sister to flamingos. So in the new world order, those two species end up next to each other in the collection.

"Familiarity with the collection also helps me when I am in the field, because I know the number and quality of all our specimens," Kristof observes. He leads expeditions all over the world to improve the Peabody's bird holdings. Five trips to Suriname, the former Dutch Guyana, have been especially productive. Kristof and his team discovered one new species for science and twelve new species for the host country among the native populations of tyrant flycatchers, antbirds, ovenbirds, tanagers, hummingbirds, and parrots.

Ornithological research trips to tropical locales like Suriname are physically demanding, as they require cutting trails and building camps in dense jungle replete with venomous snakes and other hazards. Then, long hours are devoted to finding, photographing, and sound-recording indigenous birds, setting nets to collect the birds or hunting them with shotguns, and finally skinning the birds for the trip home. (As a general rule, for each bird collected by the visiting team of scientists, a separate and equal bird is collected for scientists in the host country.) Such ventures into the wild are decidedly not Club Med–style larks. If the supply of coffee runs out after the first week, the caffeine addicts on the team suffer accordingly. If a communications satellite malfunctions, friends and family can only wonder about their loved ones for weeks at a time. Welcome to *Survivor for Scientists*.

The research facility over which Kristof presides also contains nearly 1,000 bird nests and 40,000 eggs in 10,000 individual sets. Egg collecting, now banned by law, was once a popular hobby. An Iowa farmer named Ralph W. Handsaker accumulated thousands of eggs in the early twentieth century, labeling and storing them in sawdust in cigar boxes in the attic of the family homestead. When Kristof learned of the existence of this collection, he persuaded Handsaker's heirs to donate the eggs to the Peabody. "It's a significant acquisition," he explains, "because relatively few egg specimens existed in the national collections from this part of the country, especially for grasslands species."

One of many scientists exploiting Peabody's collections for research purposes is Richard Prum, who was Kristof's advisor at Kansas. Now head curator of the Peabody's vertebrate collection (and a recent recipient of a MacArthur "genius award"), Prum digs into the collection almost daily, extracting information for the dozens of professional studies he has published on the evolution of feathers, avian phylogeny, and the underlying physics of bird colors, and the many and strange ways of bird courtship rituals.

ENCHANTED NESTS

RODERICK ROMERO IS A MANY-SPLENDORED PERSON: ARTIST, MUSICIAN (COMPOSER OF A DOZEN ALBUMS AND COUNTING FOR HIS TRANCE BAND, SKY CRIES MARY), FAMILY MAN, AND SPIRITUAL BEING WITH A SPECIAL FONDNESS FOR SAINT FRANCIS AND HIS "SISTER LARKS" AND "SISTER SWALLOWS."

But perhaps what most separates Romero from the crowd are his giant, ingeniously engineered, and beautifully crafted birds' nests for humans.

One of his most recent creations, and his first double-decker, sits, concealed by foliage, in a 150-year-old linden tree on a property with views of the Atlantic Ocean in the Hamptons. With floors made of driftwood and other recycled lumber totaling four hundred square feet, the nest is big enough to accommodate guests for cocktails and conversation. The use of gnarly vines, twigs, and branches for the walls means the nest is as close to a product of nature as one can get, "in its curves and imperfections." Not long after its completion, in fact, birds built their own nest there.

"A little bird's nest in my big nest," remarks Romero. "I was so happy they liked my work enough to build their nest there!"

Roderick grew up in Edmonds, on Puget Sound in Washington, on a woodland property thick with towering Douglas fir, maples, and cedar. He and his brothers built treehouses when they were kids, but he didn't give those experiences a second thought until 1996. A friend, Roberta Brittingham, was in the midst of creating a one-hundred-acre art installation in Bald Hills, Washington. "I wasn't even sure what I was saying," he recalls, "but I remember blurting out my vision for a big nest high in a tree where I could sleep and have tea." I was shocked when Roberta said, 'Wonderful! Do it!'"

Since then, Romero has built more than forty treehouse nests, including a unique design for Sting and his wife, Trudie Styler. "It's a kind of meditation pod," says Roderick, one in which life imitates art. "One of my assistants, who is Honduran, pointed to the pod and said, 'That looks just like the nest of the oropendola bird.' I'd never heard of the oropendola, but it became my favorite."

Those tropical birds from the blackbird family build nests that look like oblong woven baskets, three feet in length, and locate them in clusters that number from dozens to the hundreds. Romero's human version is big enough for two adults to fit inside, but it requires a very large tree to support it: the pod weighs almost four hundred pounds.

Roderick's work has been influenced by the land sculptures of the Scottish environmental artist Andy Goldsworthy and the stickwork installations of North Carolinian Patrick Dougherty. "I'd love it if my own art enjoys the same longevity," he says. Performance artist Laurie Anderson was impressed enough with his constructions to invite him to collaborate with her on an art and music piece commissioned by the pharmaceutical giant Novartis for its headquarters in Basel, Switzerland. He designed and built twelve small-scale nests to function as speakers for Anderson's "river of sound" symphonic music. "The job had to be done in three weeks," he notes, "so it was exhausting."

There is also a strong spiritual side to Romero's work. "It's like a Sufi dance, all the spinning round and round to weave the construction," he says. "It's a very birdlike process. I take a long time to pick out the right tree, and then I spend another day observing the tree, deciding on how I can locate my nest with the least amount of disturbance to the tree."

The novelist (and devoted birder) Jonathan Franzen referred to Saint Francis in an article he wrote for the *New Yorker* on the grim tradition of killing large numbers of songbirds for special meals in parts of Cyprus, Malta, and Italy. In Assisi he came upon two Franciscan sites that felt "enchanted" to him after the slaughter of birds he had witnessed.

"One was the Sacred Hut, the crude stone building in which Saint Francis and his first followers had lived in voluntary poverty and invented a brotherhood," he wrote. "The other was the tiny chapel of Santa Maria degli Angeli, outside which, in the night, as Saint Francis lay dying, his sister larks are said to have circled and sung."

While not a sacred place, the treehouse nest that Roderick Romero built gratis for the children of an East Village community in New York City is definitely enchanted. When a group of preschoolers made their first visit to the nest, perched in a willow tree, one precocious lad remarked, "Why, this is like the Guggenheim because it's round and you get to go up and up."

"That," says Romero, "was music to my ears."

PRECEDING PAGES: In a linden tree from which views of the Atlantic Ocean can be enjoyed, Roderick Romero built a double-decker nest which disappears from view when the tree leafs out. OPPOSITE: Climbing the ladder, fashioned from driftwood and reclaimed Douglas fir, to the hidden nest is a magical *Alice in Wonderland* experience for children and adults alike. ABOVE: Romero's journal is a mixture of quotidian notations, such as flight schedules and telephone numbers, and artful explorations of human figures and nests in progress.

OPPOSITE: The schoolyard nest that Roderick Romero built gratis for children in Manhattan's East Village, including his own daughter, Petra, gives the kids a much-appreciated gathering place. ABOVE: With organic curves and natural imperfections, Romero weaves his constructions the way birds might build their nests. LEFT: This particular nest was one of twelve Romero made for musician and performance artist Laurie Anderson, for use in a "river of sound" installation for Novartis in Basel, Switzerland.

HILLTOP HILTON
FOR BIRDS AND MORE

DRIVING UP THE DIRT ROAD LEADING TO INTERIOR DESIGNER DON CONNELLY'S GETAWAY FARMHOUSE, THE FIRST THING TO NOTICE IS THE DOZENS OF PURPLE MARTIN HOUSES PERCHED HIGH ON CEDAR POSTS. THE BIRDS, ANNUAL MIGRANTS FROM THE AMAZON BASIN IN SOUTH AMERICA, ARRIVE HERE IN FLATONIA, TEXAS, IN FEBRUARY, MAKE THEIR NESTS, AND RAISE THEIR YOUNG BEFORE PACKING UP AND RETURNING TO THEIR WINTERING GROUNDS IN JULY.

Whether or not they share the countrified design sensibility of their patron, the visiting birds seem to appreciate the many quirky condo-style forms the houses present. All were crafted for Connelly by Daniel Kresta, a septuagenarian neighbor who enjoys puttering around with hammer and saw even as he keeps up with his own spread.

"When the birds show up, they start scouting out the houses," Don relates. "The males arrive early, and then the females move in." A noisy summer of love ensues, with the birds chitchatting and performing their aerial maneuvers. A type of swallow, the purple martin is a voracious insectivore. "They eat mosquitoes," Don reports gratefully.

Connelly has been fascinated with animals since childhood. "My room was like a pet shop," he recalls. "I had a fish, gerbils, hamsters, you name it. And I was the kind of kid who needed to know the names for the birds I would see. Thanks to a supportive mother, I had every field guide imaginable."

The tin-roofed farmhouse has views stretching twenty miles in every direction. It is only a two-hour drive from Don's primary home in a high-rise in Houston, but a world apart in character. In fact, it is a grown-up version of Don's "pet shop" of old, filled with the things that excite a boy's imagination: wasp nests, snake skins and other remnants of natural history, and artifacts of the Old West, such as Native American pots, Navajo horse blankets, and old hunting trophies.

When Don arrives at the farm (virtually every weekend), the first thing he does is to check in with his animals, which include a small herd of cattle that he owns with a friend. "When the horses see my truck coming through the gate, they come running to see Daddy," he says of his stable of ten quarter horses. After he and the horses have become reacquainted over offerings of peppermint treats, he checks on his flock of thirty free-range old English game bantams, housed in a rustic coop that Don himself assembled from recycled materials. "Even the chicken wire came off an old turkey barn," he says.

Connelly's eighty-acre property was originally settled in 1902 by a Czech family, part of the large community of farmers that formed here after emigrating from eastern Europe in the late nineteenth century. "Even today," notes Don, "the older folks still speak Czech and dance the polka."

When Don bought the dwelling in 2000, the cottage had been unoccupied for thirty years. "The windows were all shot out, the porch was falling off, the floor was collapsing, and the house was leaning to one side," he recalls. "I remember the realtor saying, 'So when are you going to bulldoze it and put up a nice new brick house?' But I was determined to do things differently."

After he fixed up the foundation and added indoor plumbing and a wraparound porch, his dream of a farmhouse began to come true. "The place reminded me of a farm I used to visit as a child," he relates. "It was in Hempstead, outside of Houston, and belonged to the family of a friend of mine. It had a big lake and cows and lots of land, and it just made me love the experience of going to the country."

Now he enjoys that experience in full, "waking up to the crow of the rooster," he says, "and watching a mama hen scoot her chicks around the yard." Don's mother bought him a painting of baby chicks when he was seven, and it hung in his bedroom for years. Now it's come full circle, home for good on a wall in a farmhouse in Flatonia.

PRECEDING PAGES: On Don Connelly's rural property in Texas, a rustic condo community mounted on cedar posts awaits the annual spring migration of purple martins. OPPOSITE: The Mona Lisa is a nineteenth-century academic painting that "follows a visitor around with her eyes," says Don, an interior designer and owner of the Houston design shop Area. On the table is a collection of Victorian taxidermy. FOLLOWING PAGES: Neutral backgrounds and upholstery keep the living room rustic yet refined. An armless banquette-style sofa provides comfort without cluttering up the small space. The 1930's horn chair came from a Barcelona hotel lobby. Rewired, an antique French lantern illuminates a dark corner.

OPPOSITE: On the antique chest of drawers, a pair of lamps stand on ostrich-egg bases. The landscape over the chest and the painting above the bedroom door are both eighteenth-century. The primitive crucifix is from Guatemala. ABOVE: Don Connelly added a wraparound porch to make his nine-hundred-square-foot country retreat feel much more spacious. LEFT: The back porch is furnished with an old French harvest table set with tall candlesticks from Spain. It comes with a view of the chicken coop where Don keeps his flock of Old English game hens.

THE ART OF THE BIRD

ONE DAY HE'S FLYFISHING IN THE ADIRONDACKS WITH ECONOMIST PAUL VOLCKER, THE NEXT HE'S COLLECTING NEOTROPICAL BIRDS FOR YALE IN SURINAME, THE FORMER DUTCH GUYANA. WELCOME TO THE WIDE, WONDERFUL WORLD OF ARTIST, WRITER, AND NATURALIST JAMES PROSEK, ONLY IN HIS MIDTHIRTIES AND ALREADY FAMOUS FOR HIS BOOKS ON FISH AND HIS UNCONVENTIONAL PORTRAITS OF BIRDS.

When you meet James in his Connecticut home and studio, in the woodsy small town where he grew up, you have no idea of his near-celebrity status. Instead, you get the impression he is a regular, hands-in-the-pockets kind of guy, unimpressed with himself and intensely interested in everything else.

A recent self-portrait, showing James with the enormous beak of a South American toucan protruding from above his forehead, suggests the artist's penchant for departing from the norm. So, too, do his paintings of hybrid creatures such as the sailfish, depicted with a scarlet macaw's wing in place of a dorsal fin, the parrotfish with a bird beak, and the flying fox with the wings of a crow. These are radical departures from the specimen-format watercolors of fish in his acclaimed first book, *Trout: An Illustrated History*, published in 1996, when he was a twenty-year-old senior at Yale.

"I wanted to do pictures imagining that I knew less about the natural world," he explains, likening his hybrid depictions to the work of artists from earlier centuries, who based their paintings on verbal descriptions and incomplete specimens brought back by explorers of exotic lands, filling in the details with a kind of intuitive guesswork. In similar fashion he has created hybrid sculptures of what he calls "tool birds," including a stuffed starling with the nib of a fountain pen for a beak, a duck with a drill bit instead of a bill, and a cockatoo with a Swiss Army knife in place of its crest.

Edgy humor underlies much of Prosek's work. For a 2007 exhibit at the Aldrich Contemporary Art Museum, Prosek reproduced on a gallery wall in greatly magnified form the famous "roadside silhouettes" of common birds appearing in the endpapers of Roger Tory Peterson's groundbreaking field guide from the 1940s. James retained the original numbering of each bird but left off the key with the birds' identities. "The human urge is to fit everything into boxes," he observes. "I wanted to cause a little visual frustration for visitors." About the field guide, he says, "Its beauty and genius was that it provided a simple way for people to organize nature. Names serve a purpose but sometimes they make us prisoners of the official way of looking at things."

Befitting the artist's fascination with natural science both ancient and contemporary, Prosek works alternately in a newly built post-and-beam barn and in an antique studio attached to his house. The studio once served as a one-room schoolhouse in his town. James saw a truck hauling the circa-1850 structure when he himself was in elementary school; he was amazed when the schoolhouse was finally set down on a site on the street where he lived.

James's father, Louis, came to this country at age thirteen from São Paulo, Brazil. He and his brother had been avid birders, capturing small tropical species and keeping them in cages on their porch. Early on, Louis tutored his son in the pleasures and challenges of watching birds, and both Louis and James's mother, Christina, encouraged his interest in art. By the time he was nine, James was drawing birds with colored pencils, copying from pictures in Audubon's *Birds of America*. "That book spent more time on our

OPPOSITE: Sketches, reference books, and specimens from the natural world, including the tail of a bluefin tuna, inform James Prosek's body of work as well as his studio. The white bell bird was painted on location in Suriname during an expedition for Yale's Peabody Museum of Natural History. ABOVE: Other watercolors done on the Suriname trip capture the local flora and fauna, including a neotropical bird—the blue-crowned motmot—and a coral snake.

ABOVE: Parrots on another circular canvas, this one in the main house, are superimposed on a network of curvilinear lines and provide a startling welcome for visitors. ABOVE RIGHT: James Prosek with a self-portrait, also circular, incorporating the headdress of a toucan. OPPOSITE: The great blue heron, after a piece by Louis Agassiz Fuertes, is identified by Prosek not by its name but with an abstract pattern achieved by staining a portion of the canvas with tea. The sea duck, a surf scoter, was mounted on a pole, as were other specimens, for an exhibition, but without the plexiglass box. In this instance, the artist "identified" the bird with a red splotch of paint and a number.

living room table than it did in the library," he says.

Subsequently, a pal introduced him to fishing, a sport that would push birds into the background, at least temporarily. After seeing his first native brook trout, James was hooked. At age fourteen, a new mentor entered his life. "I got caught by the game warden fishing illegally in a drinking-water reservoir in our town," Prosek recalls. "But instead of giving me a ticket, he took me under his wing."

The warden, Joe Haines, was a consummate woodsman who refined the boy's fishing skills and taught him "how to find edible mushrooms or four-leaf clovers, how to catch blue crabs and find razor clams, and how to spear, skin, and cook eels." Joe also looked over the boy's shoulder as he painted fishes and offered such blunt critiques as "Brook trout tails are never forked" and "Fish don't smile."

James played sports in high school but admits he was somewhat reclusive socially. "I was always doing school work and drawing." The driven student's valedictory speech at graduation posited trout streams as a metaphor for fragility and opportunity in the habitat of life. (He still fishes in the same pond he trolled as a boy.) At Yale James pressed on intellectually and artistically. Majoring in English and architecture, he wrote his thesis on Izaak Walton of *The Compleat Angler* fame. His faculty adviser was the Compleat Literary Critic, Harold Bloom, with whom James is still friends.

"Prosek's work invites broader questions about how we obtain and process information today," wrote Shelley Langdale, associate curator of prints and

In the barn next to James Prosek's Connecticut home, an array of birds painted on sheet rock panels reproduces in magnified form the famous "Roadside Silhouettes" introduced as an identification aid in Roger Tory Peterson's field guides in the 1940s. The oil-on-board painting of three toucans is based on specimens in the Peabody Museum's vertebrate collection. *Drill Duck,* a hooded merganser with a drill bit for a beak, is part of the artist's "work bird" series.

drawings at the Philadelphia Museum of Art, for a recent exhibition of his art in Richmond, Virginia. "He skillfully navigates the line between fact and fiction, real and imagined, as he continues to probe our perceptions of nature and the inherent subjectivity of the constructs we devise in our attempt to comprehend it." Maturing as an artist, Prosek went to great lengths to capture his subjects accurately. For research on a book he is preparing on the fishes of the Atlantic Ocean, he recently went to sea with a swordfish boat out of Woods Harbour in Nova Scotia. In six days the crew harpooned thirteen swordfish, the largest measuring ten feet and weighing 250 pounds. James made sketches and took notes on this giant's "insane purple blue" back and brilliant silver sides, all of which with death would quickly fade to a bronzy-copper hue. In the studio he would try to capture the swordfish in a final rendering, "flickering with living color and light, as if lit by some internal force," as James puts it, "a swimming mirror reflecting the world around it."

Another recent adventure entailed being dropped by helicopter into the Wilhelmina mountain range in Suriname, home to the largest untouched tropical forest in the world. As a "curatorial affiliate" of Yale's Peabody Museum of Natural History, James spent three weeks working hand in hand with researchers, including Kristof Zyskowski, manager of the Peabody's vertebrate collection. The team collected birds, recorded birdsongs, and dodged poisonous snakes. At night, the tireless seekers of knowledge set up a white sheet on a hoop and illuminated it with a mercury vapor light.

"We were trying to attract the white witch moth, which has the largest wingspan of any insect—twelve and a half inches across," James explains. "We caught five in the time we were there. We tried to get them to lay eggs, because no one has ever seen the caterpillar of the species, but we failed." James pauses, then utters the signature sign-off of the Compleat Naturalist: "Maybe next time."

FURNISHING THE NEST:
COLLECTING WITH AN AVIAN THEME

LIKE BIRDERS, COLLECTORS COME IN ALL STRIPES. SOME PEOPLE COLLECT PIECES IN ONE MATERIAL, SUCH AS WOOD OR SILVER. OTHERS LIMIT THEIR COLLECTIONS TO THE WORK OF A SINGLE MAKER, SUCH AS WEDGWOOD OR FABERGÉ. PERHAPS THE MAJORITY OF PEOPLE WHO COLLECT ARE DRIVEN BY THEME. ANYTHING THAT BEARS THE DESIRED IMAGE, WHETHER IT'S BOTANICALS, HEARTS, DOGS, OR OWLS, IS ELIGIBLE FOR A PLACE OF HONOR IN THE HOME.

Birders are de facto collectors. As Donal O'Brien, a former longtime chair of the Audubon Society, has said, "Birding is like catch-and-release hunting." The birder sights a bird, takes a mental snapshot of it, or a more literal digital image of it, and moves on to the next species. Birders also tend to amass field guides and other tomes on natural history. Some collect more binoculars than they will ever have a need for, like golfers who keep adding putters to their bags.

Kathryn and Geoffrey Precourt were collectors long before they met and married, and they have doubled down on that passion since their wedding day. As a result, their house in western Massachusetts today is a treasure trove of antiques and collectibles, many with a birding theme.

"I've been watching birds ever since I was a Girl Scout," says Kathryn. "I loved feathers for their softness and patterns and was always on the lookout for them. I made friends with one of the keepers at the Houston Zoo, and he would save the peacock feathers for me that he found on the grounds."

The Precourt abode is brimming with all forms of avian life in imagined form. There are antique prints of birds, bird silhouettes, schoolgirl watercolors of birds, feather paintings, Victorian taxidermy, bird drawings, cocktail napkins with roosters on them, China patterns with birds, water pitchers shaped like toucans, and whatever else a trip to the flea market or a search on eBay might yield.

"The thing is," says Kathryn, "I didn't even know I had been collecting all these birds until I started going through the house. I was amazed at what a flock we had."

The Precourts' collecting habit provides a useful idea file for those birders who wish to bring their enthusiasm for birds into their own homes. Their collection ranges from the affordable to the rare. Kathryn filled a vintage store fixture with ephemera she found at flea markets—cigarette cards, photos, post-cards, valentines, and other greeting cards. "I never paid more than five dollars for a single item," she says.

The Chinese "rank badges" that the Precourts recently have begun to collect are in another price range altogether. "I first spotted them at an antiques show and was immediately drawn to them because of the incredible handwork and the story each badge told," she recalls.

The woven or embroidered silk squares were once worn on the front and back of surcoats as a symbol of status and achievement in pre-communist China. Male recruits of all ages underwent exams to enter into service to the emperor. Military ranks bore images of mythical creatures like dragons. Civilian ranks were represented by birds, listed in order of superiority:

1. cranes
2. golden pheasant
3. peacock
4. wild goose
5. silver pheasant
6. egret
7. mandarin duck
8. quail
9. paradise flycatcher

"In Chinese lore," says Kathryn, "cranes are at the top of the class because they symbolize longevity and wisdom, but even the paradise flycatcher sounds like a good score to me."

PRECEDING PAGES: In a tiny bedroom, bluebirds of happiness inspire a classic blue-and-white decorating scheme. "It's such a small space," says Kathryn Precourt, "I needed it to stay crisp and airy." OPPOSITE, ABOVE: English transferware, often with an avian theme, is a product of the nineteenth-century Aesthetic Movement and makes a nice resting place for a folk art bird. OPPOSITE, BELOW: Flourishings of the birds in antique gold frames date from the nineteenth century. ABOVE: The price is right for inexpensive ephemera like cigarette cards, early photos, Victorian postcards and vintage calling cards, all of which can be found with images of birds on them.

OPPOSITE: In the dining room, walls are decorated with mostly eighteenth- and nineteenth-century art illustrating various stages in the life of a bird. An artist who executed murals for New York's Museum of Natural History did the painting on the wall, above a papier mâché plate from the nineteenth century. TOP: This painterly image of a bird, a nineteenth-century German work, was actually made with feathers. ABOVE: A pair of English nineteenth-century silver luster pitchers are decorated with birds.

TOP: A shelf in the entry hall holds a nineteenth-century watercolor of a bird and an antique foot warmer. ABOVE: A collection of early twentieth-century bird pitchers from Czechoslovakia, Bavaria, Germany, and Japan got its start with the tiny pitcher Kathryn acquired as a girl. OPPOSITE: The library boasts a collection of Chinese rank badges, hand-embroidered on silk and various eighteenth-century French bird prints, from Panteek.

RULES FOR COLLECTING

- Collect by theme. Remember that owl collection of Great-Aunt Mary? You'll find that birds are everywhere once you start focusing your gaze. Just be careful what you wish for!

- Pick a time period you like, such as the 1940s and '50s. "There are a lot of fun things for the midcentury collector," says Kathryn Precourt. "Look for '50s lamps with bird bases. There's always a place for bark cloth and pink flamingos."

- Pick a medium you like, such as textiles. "Birds were a dominant design motif in vintage fabrics. Think peacocks and songbirds. "Look for damaged fabric at the flea market," she suggests. "It's going to be a lot cheaper than fabric in good condition, and that hole or tear isn't going to make a difference once it's cut up to make a cover for a throw pillow."

- Pay your price, not theirs. Finding something at the right cost is part of the fun of collecting. "Do your homework and come armed with knowledge," advises Kathryn.

- Go online. "eBay, Etsy, and 1stdibs are my favorite online sources for collecting birdy things," says Kathryn. Keep the search narrow for best results—name that bird!

- Look for birdy bling. "Birds are a popular motif in costume jewelry," says Kathryn. "Flea markets and tag sales usually have plenty to choose from. Wear a whole flock of bird pins on your vest."

- Don't judge the book by its cover. Birds are a favorite subject in vintage children's books. Don't pass by a book just because the cover is in bad shape. Illustrated pages inside the book may be suitable for framing.

- For birds on paper, you can't beat an ephemera show or a postcard show.

PART III

AT HOME WITH BIRDS

Home is where the heart of the birder is. Here is where bird enthusiasts draw on the centuries-old traditions of avian arts, crafts, and design to decorate their personal nests in individual and often iconoclastic ways. Lovers of birds live it up in a style that would do a peacock proud.

SHOREBIRDS UNLIMITED

WITH WILLOWY, ATHLETIC GRACE, ADELAIDE SKOGLUND GLIDES THROUGH HER FLORIDA KEYS HOME, WHERE A COLLECTION OF CARVED AND PAINTED BIRDS ATTESTS TO HER PASSION FOR WILDLIFE. THE LIFELONG FISHER, HUNTER, AND GOLFER IS ALWAYS ON THE GO. A CALL FROM HER FAVORITE FISHING GUIDE, WITH NEWS THAT THE TARPON ARE RUNNING, IMMEDIATELY BRINGS AN ALTERATION IN HER SOCIAL CALENDAR. LUNCH WITH A GOOD FRIEND IS OFF. CHANGING INTO FLY FISHING GEAR AND MEETING THE GUIDE AT THE DOCK IS ON.

An hour later, as they are cruising the warm, crystalline waters of the bonefish flats near Key Largo, a migrating warbler alights on the boat to catch its breath after a long journey from Mexico. Adelaide considers this a favorable omen, and, indeed, not much later, she hooks into her first tarpon of the day.

"The birds that live near water are the ones I'm most familiar with," she says. "When I'm fishing, I always see herons, which are themselves the best fishers in the world. In the spring, tired migratory warblers show up in the trees around the house. I've also watched a merlin pick off warblers, flying with such speed from its perch on a dead tree at Curtis Point, a place where we go for tarpon."

PRECEDING PAGES: Adelaide Skoglund drew on her collections of shorebird art and blue-and-white export china to devise a decorating scheme for her waterside home in the Florida Keys. ABOVE: Renderings of the black-necked stilt, with its very long red legs, and the species of plover called killdeer make an attractive pairing. OPPOSITE: Herons and pelicans are everyday sights in the Keys.

Out west, where she fishes every summer on the ranch of her friend and fellow art collector Bill Legg, Adelaide enjoys sightings of eagles and hawks and, recently, a family of great horned owls in a grove of cottonwoods on Bill's land.

Growing up in the Piedmont region of North Carolina, Adelaide learned how to fish and hunt from her father, a passionate outdoorsman who owned a horse farm in the country. As a girl, she pulled bass from the farm pond and followed bird dogs, trained by her dad, in pursuit of quail in the fields and woods surrounding the farm.

"My father loved birds, too, and instilled that enthusiasm in me," she says. "We had bird feeders all over the farm. Birds and fish have a lot in common, I think, but birds make better art."

Adelaide and her husband, John, who died in 1999, began collecting avian art in the 1980s, when they lived in Minnesota. "If we liked it, we bought it," she notes. "We were not consciously building a collection, but that's what happened. We would leave walls bare until we had just the right piece of art for the space."

Much more space became available when they built the house on Card Sound in Florida, incorporating features in the design that accommodated their art and made the most of the waterside location. A mahogany bar between the living room and family room was cleverly designed to serve guests both inside the house and outside on the spacious veranda overlooking the swimming pool and deck. Carved birds and collections of blue-and-white Chinese ceramics are on display in cabinets and on shelves also fashioned from West Indies mahogany, a traditional building material in the Caribbean. (Today mahogany is in scarce supply and rarely available.)

The exotic wood is a dark accent in what is largely a bright and cheerful white interior with splashes of blue. "It was hard to find the right blue," she relates. "I didn't want a harsh navy blue or a soft powder blue, but something in between." She picked out most of the furniture, antiques, and art, adding, "I didn't want a decorated house, I wanted my house."

ABOVE: Roseate spoonbills are portrayed in a Florida Keys setting, although today a decline in their main food source, oysters and shrimp, has forced the birds to relocate farther north. OPPOSITE: Enthralled with the appearance and behavior of birds that live near the water, Adelaide has collected many likenesses of birds in diverse forms, such as the carved kingfisher on the table between armchairs, made by John Kobald, a Colorado fishing guide. The portrait of a lone gull by the renowned Raymond Ching (right back wall), a New Zealand artist now living and working in England, hangs above a wildlife drama depicting two eagles fighting over a snake, a work in lapis lazuli found in an airport shop.

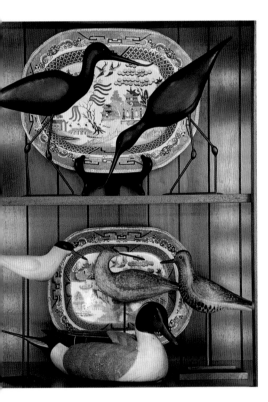

ABOVE: The pair of avocets, a mud-dwelling species with an unusual upturned bill, were carved by Ronnie Riddle. The pintail duck and shorebirds on the lower shelf are by Mark McNair, a Virginia carver considered one of the best at work today. ABOVE RIGHT: The avid sportswoman on her classically designed porch overlooking Card Sound, with friends. OPPOSITE: The carved figures of five curlew, along with the blue herons flanking the sofa, are all by Mark McNair.

Some of Adelaide's favorite images in the home, such as the painting of roseate spoonbills in a guest bathroom, or the Frank Benson etching of a brown pelican in the living room, are familiar species to Floridians. So are most of the carved shorebirds in Adelaide's spacious, "ducks unlimited" kitchen, where no fewer than thirty figures of water birds watch over the nightly preparations for dinner.

Benson was a noted plein air painter in the early twentieth century. Much of the art Adelaide has collected, however, is contemporary. In one of her favorite sitting areas in the house, a pair of blue herons flank five curlews arranged as a flock on a table. All were made by Mark McNair, considered one of the finest carvers working today. McNair sculpts his creations in a rural Virginia town on the Eastern Shore, an area traditionally associated with decoy carving. In fact, early in his career, McNair repainted some of the decoys of an earlier master, Ira Hudson, but he discontinued restoration work when he discovered dealers were passing off his pieces as original Hudsons.

Bird carving has evolved as an art form since the market gunning era of the late nineteenth and early twentieth centuries. At that time, rigs of duck and goose decoys were produced in large quantities for use by hunters. Killing ducks, geese, and shorebirds to supply fast-growing American cities with game meat became a lucrative industry and led to alarming reductions in wildlife populations. Public outrage caused Congress to pass the Migratory Bird Treaty Act in 1918, outlawing market gunning and placing limits on bird hunting for sport. Ten years later, a second piece of legislation made the shooting of any shorebird illegal.

As a result of decreased demand for decoys, many carvers switched to other fields of endeavor. "However, a few craftsmen whose output was most highly regarded turned to the carving and painting of birds not only in full but also in partial or miniature sizes," writes Joseph H. Ellis in *Birds in Wood and Paint*. "These were sold to buyers who appreciated them from both an artistic and a natural-history point of view rather than because of their ability to lure their living counterparts."

Ellis, a retired partner of Goldman Sachs and a lifelong birder, identifies two Massachusetts carvers, Elmer Crowell of East Harwich and Joseph W. Lincoln of Accord, as the progenitors of what became known as "decorative" carvings with folk art qualities. These are some of the works that have caught the eye of Adelaide Skoglund over the years. Indeed, she recently acquired several Crowell shorebirds at auction, at what she thinks were bargain prices.

"My stepdaughter, Holly Frank, who is an interior designer in New York, sometimes tells me I have too much stuff," Adelaide laughs. "But I always think there's room for one more thing."

THE EGGS AND US

PAUL MROZINSKI VIVIDLY RECALLS HIS FIRST VISIT TO THE ARIZONA DESERT, WHICH OCCURRED WHILE HE WAS ATTENDING ARCHITECTURE SCHOOL AT ARIZONA STATE UNIVERSITY IN THE 1960S. "I GREW UP IN THE INNER CITY OF CHICAGO," HE NOTES. "THERE WERE NO BIRDS THERE." SO WHEN HE NOTICED THE HOLES BIRDS HAD BORED INTO THE TRUNKS AND LARGER BRANCHES OF THE GIANT SAGUAROS, HE WAS IMPRESSED. TO A STUDENT OF STRUCTURE, THE TOWERING CACTUS WAS A MULTI-STORIED APARTMENT COMPLEX WITH MANY BIRDS LIVING IN CLOSE PROXIMITY AND MOVING IN AND OUT CONSTANTLY.

"This is when I really began to appreciate nature," says Paul. "I realized there was much to be learned from observing birds, their behavior, and the way they build nests. After all, birds don't have the option of shopping at the lumberyard. They have to work with what they find in their native habitat."

Paul's wife, Sharon, got much more familiar with the desert environment growing up in Arizona. "I was out in nature all the time," she relates. "I too was fascinated by the birds that build nests and lay their eggs inside and on some of the arms of a prickly cactus. I love structure and design, so I always paid attention to the way birds' nests were put together."

PRECEDING PAGES: The portrait of Sharon and her mother was painted by Maine artist Anna B. McCoy, while the farmer-grown gourds were picked out by Sharon for their birdlike aspect.
ABOVE: The Shaker design esthetic of the homeowners makes for a simple yet authentic room style with an emphasis on the gifts of nature. The scarecrow painting is by a friend. OPPOSITE, ABOVE LEFT: A bonanza of eggs in boxes was discovered at a Maine antiques auction. OPPOSITE, ABOVE RIGHT: The avian mystique casts its spell everywhere in the house. OPPOSITE, BELOW: A folk art bird made of tarpaper struts its stuff.

Today, Sharon and Paul split their time between their eighteenth-century Wiscasset, Maine, home, filled with antique textiles and furnishings and incorporating their antiques business, the Marston House, and the south of France, where they do most of their buying for the business. They also operate a small bed-and-breakfast on the Wiscasset property.

Their Maine home is infused with the spirit and style of an avid nineteenth-century naturalist, with many collections centered on aspects of avian life. Eggs are everywhere. "They're the most perfect form in nature," says Sharon. "The egg is another form of home." There are also nests aplenty in the couple's Wiscasset home such as those once used for teaching purposes in the nineteenth century, complete with their original handwritten identification labels.

The living birds the couple see, both here and abroad, bring them the greatest pleasure. "Birds catch my eye," says Sharon. "I always know when a newcomer visits my garden to drink at the make-do birdbath or to feed on our berries or fruit trees."

PRECEDING PAGES: Lithographs of eggs on the wall and miniature antique paintings of birds on the mantel help to make the bedroom truly feel like a place of contemplation and rest. ABOVE: Paul and Sharon Mrozinski divide their time between the south of France and Wiscasset, Maine, where they have an antiques shop and a small bed-and-breakfast. OPPOSITE: In the vestibule, a Swedish pine clock built in the early nineteenth century features on its face painted flourishes of feathers, used to separate the Roman numerals.

Sharon's favorite bird is the crow. She has a folk sculpture of a crow made from roofing material and a lifelike scarecrow that artist friends made for Sharon as a going-away gift when she and Paul moved from California to Maine. "The scarecrow was dressed in overalls and a hat," relates Sharon. "I put him in the garden next to the mudroom door of our shop. He quickly became the source of much commentary."

One artist friend of theirs in particular became so fascinated with the scarecrow that Sharon finally sent him home with it. Time passed. Periodically the artist called to report, "That scarecrow keeps turning into a human. But I want it to be a crow!" A few years later, at Christmas, the artist returned the scarecrow, and with it he brought a watercolor he had painted of the crow, inscribed to the Mrozinskis. The human-size scarecrow figure had finally turned into a full-fledged *Corvus brachyrhynchos*.

Ever since she was a child, admits Sharon, "I have admired crows for their cleverness. They not only use tools, they make them, turning sticks or bits of metal into probes and hooks." She notes, "I have seen them count and known them to recognize people. They are such curious and social creatures. A large flock watches over our home and awakens our bed-and-breakfast guests."

MENAGERIE À DEUX

STEP INTO THE URBAN LOFT OF HIPSTER SISTERS HOLLISTER AND PORTER HOVEY AND ENTER A WORLD THAT GETS CURIOUSER AND CURIOUSER. THE TWENTY-FIRST-CENTURY ANTIQUARIANS WITH AN UNERRING EYE FOR FASHION AND DESIGN HAVE FILLED THEIR HOME, IN THE WILLIAMSBURG SECTION OF BROOKLYN, NEW YORK, WITH A VANISHING SPECIES OF ACCOUTREMENTS. "WE'RE DEFINITELY MORE GATHERER THAN HUNTER," DECLARES HOLLISTER ABOUT THE VINTAGE TAXIDERMY SURROUNDING HER. "WE'VE NEVER SHOT A THING!"

The Hovey women are part of a young design movement, defined by authenticity and love of nature, which they believe took shape following the tumultuous events of 9/11.

"We came to New York in 2000," explains Hollister. "A year later, with the attack on the twin towers, many people here suddenly lost all interest in the superficial or throwaway." When the sisters moved in together in 2005, they created their own den of found objects: a swan that once served as a prop in a window of Harry Winston hibernates in an old pharmacy cabinet; warblers of the Christmas-tree-ornament variety nest in a chandelier; a pheasant hovers in midflight over a mantel. "This is our way of being in touch with the natural world before it all disappears," says Hollister in a tone that is both flip and sardonic. "Everything is either vanishing or going to be lost."

The sisters' parents met in New York in the early 1970s, when their father, Porter, was working at the World Trade Center and their mother, Lana, was an assistant editor at *Mademoiselle.* Porter Hovey had by then satisfied his wanderlust, managing a gold mine in Bolivia, supervising the shipment of a boat filled with cattle to the Philippines, and relaxing on an Afrikaner farm near Cape Town in the summer of 1967. The Hovey girls themselves grew up in less exotic conditions in the American Midwest. "Our mother wanted to be closer to her dad and her roots when she had kids," says Hollister. When the girls were five and one, the family moved from Lincoln, Nebraska, to Kansas City, Kansas. "Our dad looked at Kansas City as another adventure," she laughs.

Their maternal grandfather instilled in them an appreciation for nature when they were tots. "Our grandpa taught us how to fish." Porter recalls, "He'd take us fishing at the lake by his home so we could catch trout and catfish. He pointed out birds to us, explained the habits of different species, and imitated their songs by whistling."

Porter, a photographer, works for a management consultant firm, and Hollister is a director at a medical public relations firm. Both are ardent bloggers. As the unabashed romantic of the two, Porter devotes her blog (kisssing. blogspot.com) to love . . . and kisses. "There is this wonderful picture of my parents on their wedding day, midkiss, that started it all for me," says Porter. "They were so young and dashing and ridiculously goofy." Her blog is a visual commentary on love found and love lost. "The photos all show these moments

of great poignancy or happiness, but as modern-day viewers, the audience understands how fleeting those moments can be. More than half the couples on my blog ended up in divorce court! But they were truly happy at one time, and it's great to immortalize that feeling—even if it couldn't last."

Hollister's blog (hollisterhovey.blogspot.com) offers keenly observed posts on fashion, art, music, travel, books, and design, and mines the lost grandeur of generations past (think expeditions, costume balls, Yale-Harvard football games, the sporting life).

"Mom was always dragging her girls around to flea markets," says Hollister. "We grew up wearing old Ralph Lauren cricket jackets, boys' oxfords, and other classic preppy fare that our mom found. Our father mowed the lawn in a pith helmet and wore the same pair of tassel loafers as long as we can remember."

The DNA didn't fall far from the tree. "We love flea markets too, and the local Brooklyn junk shops and eBay," notes Porter. "Practically everything in our apartment once had another life. It's all about creating a place of permanence in a city full of transients. The taxidermy makes us feel in touch with nature. The mounted trophies are like friends. We give them all names."

Finding interesting taxidermy is one thing; getting it back home is another. "New Yorkers have seen it all," says Hollister, "but they still act severely shocked when they see a gal carrying a merino sheep's head through Grand Central Station."

OPPOSITE: As twenty-first-century mixologists, the Hovey sisters have stocked their bar with small-batch spirits, artisanal bitters, flasks and hunt cups, a tintype portrait, a bust in an old fencing mask and, overseeing all, a print of a golden eagle, found in a bookstore in Prague. ABOVE: The swan, acquired through a posting on Craigslist, was originally a prop in the New York storefront of Harry Winston. For atmosphere, the Hoveys added stalks of cotton left over from a frontier-themed party they hosted.

ABOVE: Flaunting convention as always, Hollister Hovey found the 1967 folding Raleigh bicycle on e-Bay and pedaled it all the way home from Harlem wearing velvet slippers. The gull on the industrial stool is made of papier-mâché.
OPPOSITE: Taking up residence in the chandelier, a flock of Christmas ornaments convey a year-round feeling of cheer and goodwill toward birds.

DRESSED TO BIRD

FOR THE BIRDING FASHIONISTA:
WHAT TO WEAR NOW

HAT: For the Miss Jane Hathaway look, try on a pith helmet (eBay.com) or discover your inner explorer with a Tilley LTM5A Airflo Nylamtium Audubon hat (tilley.com), the headgear of choice of Canadian soldiers.

SHIRT: Feel like you're walking in Roger Tory Peterson's shadow in an authentic bush shirt of 100 percent Italian cotton poplin from F.M. Allen (fmallen.com), the firm with the slogan "East Africa 1947."

PANTS: Pull on a pair of trekking pants by the Swedish outfitter Fjällräven (fjallraven.com) and head for the Ramble in Central Park.

JACKET: The tin cloth field jacket by Seattle, Washington, outdoor clothing specialist Filson (ccfilson .com) wears like iron with plenty of pockets for stowing an iPod loaded with birdsong apps or energy bars.

SHOES: Boot up with the Vasque Sundowner (vasque.com) or the Diemme New Tirol (chcmshop.com) and follow your "spark" bird up city canyons and through the woods.

RUCKSACK: Strap on a classic waxed cotton field bag by L.L. Bean (llbean .com) designed for the avid birder with pockets sized for binoculars and guidebooks. Pack a soft-cover journal. Ernest Hemingway reputedly penned pages of *The Sun Also Rises* in his Moleskine (moleskine.com). Record your life list in yours.

DON'T FORGET THE SOUVENIRS: In New York City, Hollister Hovey and her sister, Porter, recommend taking home a decoupage by the artist John Derian (johnderian.com), who uses eighteenth-century engravings of birds, feathers, and nests to decorate his plates and platters, or they suggest picking out a curiosity of the Victorian taxidermy kind found at Obscura (obscuraantiques.com) or Darr (shopdarr.com).

FLIGHT OF FANCY

I STILL REMEMBER THE FIRST BIRD BOOK I HAD AS A CHILD. IT HAD THIS PICTURE OF A BALTIMORE ORIOLE'S NEST THAT AMAZED ME AT THE TIME," SAYS HOUSTON ANTIQUES DEALER KAY O'TOOLE. OBLONG IN SHAPE AND TIGHTLY WOVEN OF PLANT MATERIALS, THE ORIOLE'S NEST CAN EASILY PASS FOR A BOHEMIAN DESIGNER POUCH. "MAYBE THAT'S WHAT GOT ME INTERESTED IN NESTS IN THE FIRST PLACE," SAYS KAY. "I STILL HAVEN'T ACTUALLY SEEN A BALTIMORE ORIOLE, BUT I SURE DO REMEMBER THE NEST."

Her mother's passion for birds was infectious. "I became so much more aware of birds because of my mother." Kay relates, "There were a half-dozen feeders in our yard and always a pair of binoculars on the table in our family room. She adored tufted titmice and hummingbirds because they were so tiny, like herself."

Hidden away like a bird's nest is Kay's own home, a surprise to all who happen upon it, sequestered behind her shop at the corner of a busy commercial street in Houston. Its design is based on the style of an eighteenth-century French Quarter house Kay saw in a book about historic architecture. "You can't help but think of the Renaissance architect Palladio when you start to do something classical like this," explains Kay. The footprint of her house is one room deep with front and back windows that are mirror images of each other. "I wanted to create a European look. I like the feeling of openness that results when a lot of space is kept between things."

PRECEDING PAGES: Birds and other surprises, such as saintly gold crowns and glazed white terracotta pieces make their presence felt in Kay O'Toole's elegant living room. A bronze nest sculpture by Lisa Ludwig (see page 105) is suspended above a Peruvian painting of the Virgin Mary flanked by two antique portraits of St. Barbara. The antique low table has a lacquered surface inlaid with Chinoiserie pattern. The Italian armchair and sofa pillows are covered in Fortuny fabric; slipcovers are made of hand-woven linen from France. ABOVE: In the kitchen, next to confit jars and French creamware, the French bust of a general goes around with a cheep on its shoulder.

As for the things themselves, "Everything in the house has touched me in some way," she says, such as the birds' nests she tucks among the fine antiques and furnishings, religious artifacts and art, themselves displayed as little crown jewels.

A bird's nest is like a Rorschach test of who lives there, as revealing of its species as its song or plumage. In their book, *Egg & Nest*, Rosamond Purcell, Linnea S. Hall, and René Corado write: "Birds will use nearly all available items that fit in their 'search image' for appropriate nesting materials. Before humans manufactured items that birds could incorporate into their nests, plant and animal materials were most commonly used in nest-making. Today we are much more likely to find nests containing all manner of synthetic fibers that mimic natural materials."

One of Kay's favorite nests, beribboned with a long, slender strand of dried grass, was a gift to her. It rests in the palm of a carved saint's hand. "It's this thing I have about birds and how they go about creating a home. I can't even remember a time when I didn't have a nest in my home." Years ago Kay spotted a collection of antique specimen eggs on a buying trip to Brimfield, Massachusetts. In the box with the eggs was the tiniest nest with bits of down worked into it. "It really makes you appreciate how exquisite these works of nature are," says Kay.

Nowadays, chickens spark her imagination. Kay was watching a documentary film on the fashion designer Yves Saint Laurent. In one scene he is shown fitting Catherine Deneuve for a suit, while the actress chatters on and on about her brood of chickens. At one point she exclaims, "I just love the way they look on the lawn!" That just did it for Kay, who now keeps her own feathered lawn ornaments, Sylvia and Georgina, in a backyard folly fit for fancy hens.

TOP: Antique French birdcages were crafted with an architect's sensibility.
ABOVE: The carved wood hand of a Santos figure holds a form of woven art from nature.

OPPOSITE Elements such as pilasters were incorporated in the house, which Kay designed with architect Kirby Mears, for their classical note. The nineteenth-century Venetian bench provides a bibliophile's perch. ABOVE: Generous windows, retrieved from an old mansion slated for demolition, allow an ivied wall to be appreciated from within the house. A classic fireplace with limestone mantel was found in France. Kay's shy Italian greyhound, Sici, adds its own graceful presence.

WARBLER CAPITAL
OF THE WORLD

BIRDING GURU KENN KAUFMAN MIGRATED FROM
ARIZONA TO OHIO A FEW YEARS AGO TO LEARN MORE
ABOUT MIGRANTS—THE BIRDS THAT DESCEND IN VAST NUM-
BERS ON THE MARSHES AND WOODLANDS ALONG THE SOUTH-
ERN COAST OF LAKE ERIE EVERY SPRING AND FALL.

That's his official story. Actually, it was more a case of *cherchez la femme* than
cherchez les oiseaux. In 2001, Kenn had met Kimberly Fredritz, the education
director of Black Swamp Bird Observatory (BSBO), headquartered at Magee
Marsh Wildlife Area near Port Clinton, Ohio.

"We met at a nature and bird festival in South Texas," Kenn recalls. "Kim
was an attendee, on her first major trip outside of Ohio, and I was one of the
speakers on the program."

Subsequently, Kim invited Kenn to come to Ohio to give a talk for the tenth
anniversary of BSBO, which was celebrated in 2003.

"I spoke at their Saturday night banquet, and the following morning I led a
group of about thirty on a birding trip through a city park." Kenn relates, "It
was February, and there was lots of snow on the ground. I remember trying to
think of interesting things to point out, as we walked along, and then I got hit
with a snowball in the back of the head."

Kaufman remembers turning around and seeing the shocked expressions on
the faces of the birders. "They were afraid I was going to be deeply offended by
the assault," he says. "But instead I bent down and made a snowball of my own,
as did some others, and it immediately developed into a raging snowball fight."

PRECEDING PAGES: Tiny insects called midges breed abundantly in the spring in the marshes near Lake Erie, providing "a supercharged food supply," in the words of ornithologist Kenn Kaufman, for the waves of songbird migrants arriving at this time. ABOVE: Kaufman trades birding tall tales with Tom Bartlett, a retired biology teacher who has been "pole-sitting," as he calls it, for more than 15 years to raise money for Black Swamp Bird Observatory. ABOVE RIGHT: "I sincerely believe more warbler photographs are taken in northwest Ohio in the month of May," says Kaufman, "than in all the rest of the country." High-tech optics have made photography a popular hobby for many birders.

Later, Kenn learned it was Kim who had launched the snowball that started the battle. "Yes," he says, "that made her quite memorable, and before long I decided to move to Ohio to be near her. And soon after that, we got married."

It is no less true, though, that Kenn did want to learn as much as he could about bird migration. "For years it was something I glimpsed from a distance," he says. "The Arizona desert was fine for many natural history pursuits, but bird migration there was muted and subtle." Short trips to migrant hotspots like Cape May, New Jersey, and High Island, Texas, broadened his understanding of migration, but relocating to a hotspot of his own, Magee Marsh, proved to be the most illuminating.

"After five spring seasons in the area, I am still in awe of the migration here, and just getting to the point where I can describe it," says Kenn. Increasingly involved in BSBO, of which Kim is now executive director, he has expounded on the phenomenon of migrating birds in the Lake Erie area in lectures, blogs, and magazine articles. Kaufman delineates three basic routes for migrant birds entering the United States in the spring:

- Birds from the Caribbean and South America come through Florida, then fan out to the west as they travel toward Canada.
- Birds from Mexico's Yucatán Peninsula fly across the Gulf of Mexico, making landfall anywhere between western Florida and eastern Texas, before fanning out east and west as they move northward.
- Birds wintering in mainland Mexico fly an overland route around the Gulf, then spread eastward; many settle in eastern Canada for the breeding season.

ABOVE, CLOCKWISE FROM TOP LEFT: Among dozens of warbler species invading Ohio air space in the spring are (clockwise from top left) the yellow-rumped warbler, the blackpoll warbler, the Cape May warbler, the black-throated green warbler, and the Blackburnian warbler.

ABOVE: After a migrating bird is caught up in a do-no-harm "mist net," it is quickly weighed, measured, sexed, and banded, then released back into the wild. Joe Komorowski, a volunteer from Petersburg, Michigan, has been banding birds for more than sixteen years.

The migrating birds along all three entry routes spread out and intermingle, so that by the time they reach the Great Lakes, they are a mixed flock numbering in the hundreds of thousands. Arriving at Lake Erie, the birds are exhausted and hungry. Before tackling the flight across the lake, many descend on Magee Marsh, to ingest protein from the annual spring population explosion of insects called midges. The mile-long boardwalk that meanders through the preserve gives birders an extraordinary opportunity for viewing migrant birds, including dozens of warbler species, up close and personal. Preoccupation with foraging makes the birds virtually oblivious to people who may be standing only a few feet away from them. In 2009, a single golden-winged warbler was seen by approximately one thousand birders in a single day, according to a guide who was on the scene.

"I seriously believe that during the month of May, more warbler photographs are taken in northwestern Ohio," adds Kaufman, "than in all the rest of the United States combined."

We visited Magee Marsh in mid-May of 2010 when "The Biggest Week in American Birding," sponsored by BSBO, lured thousands of birders to the shores of Lake Erie. Over the ten-day span of the festival, Kaufman gave talks on nine evenings, led birders on tours, and was a seemingly constant presence on the boardwalk, answering questions, conversing with friends, autographing copies of his field guides, and quickly raising his binoculars whenever a winged creature flitted by in the surrounding woods.

When a visitor remarked to Kaufman on the diversity of the birders that packed the boardwalk over one weekend, he replied, "There's a perception, even in the birding community, that the average birdwatcher is wealthy, white, and retired. But more and more families, young people, and teenagers are discovering the activity."

Among the many "Biggest Week on Twitter" postings seen on the giant monitor in the BBSO registration tent was one that hinted at birding's changing demographics. The tweet read: "Sam Hinkle, age 4, nailed his first golden-winged warbler at the Magee Marsh boardwalk. Well done, buddy!"

LICENSE TO BIRD

The spring migration of warblers and other birds to the shores of Lake Erie attracts thousands of out-of-state visitors every year. A walk through the parking lot at Magee Marsh confirms that many of the nation's birders wear their hearts on their cars.

BIRDS BY DESIGN:
THE GENIUS OF CHARLEY HARPER

T HE CRAMPED STUDIO WHERE CHARLEY HARPER TURNED

OUT IMAGE AFTER IMAGE OF BIRDS AND OTHER WILDLIFE

FOR NEARLY A HALF CENTURY IS STILL A MESS. PENS AND PEN-

CILS, SQUEEZED-TO-DEATH TUBES OF PAINT, SCRAPS OF PAPER,

NEWSPAPER AND MAGAZINE CLIPPINGS, AND OTHER DEBRIS

FILL EVERY SQUARE INCH OF WORK SURFACE.

The studio is part of a modernist compound built in a woodsy suburb of Cincinnati, Ohio, in 1958, connected by a boardwalk to a house with a huge painted likeness of a ladybug on the facade. "We left it the way he left it," says Charley's son, Brett Harper, who carries on the artistic tradition of his father and his mother, Edie Harper. "Dad worked in that studio from 7:00 a.m. to midnight," he recalls. "We got him to come for dinner by pressing a buzzer that sounded in the studio."

Perhaps fittingly, when Harper died in 2007, the next work he was planning to undertake was a portrait of the possibly extinct ivory-billed woodpecker on its nest, with gremlin-looking fledglings. "He'd already stretched the canvas for it," notes Brett.

Charley Harper was born in 1922 and grew up on a farm in West Virginia, but was not taken with the conditions of rural life. For someone who developed a keen appreciation of the natural world, he had a powerful antipathy for cleaning chicken coops and working in the hay fields. He was expected to take over his father's feed store when he grew up; instead, he escaped to Ohio and the Art

Academy of Cincinnati. Jobs in advertising ensued, but freelance assignments allowed him to develop what fashion designer Todd Oldham, today a major collector responsible for the renewed interest in Harper's art, called "his lyrically joyous style." In 2007, Oldham, a fan of Harper's work since childhood, released his own monograph on Harper and his "precise futuristic birds," titled *Charley Harper: An Illustrated Life.*

"Dad's style jelled in the 1950s, when the art director at Ford Motor Company's *Ford Times* magazine asked him to draw a scene with a bird feeding station," says Brett. "Dad replied, 'I don't know what that is, but if you send me one I'll give it a try.'" That image, *Feeding Station* (1954), inspired reader requests for print copies. With help from Edie, who mixed the paint colors, Charley produced the prints in a crude basement operation. He sold them for $4.95 plus 50 cents postage.

In fact, Harper was not and never would be much of a birder (although his home grounds remain dotted with feeders). As he once famously remarked, "I do all my bird watching in field guides." Nevertheless, his keen perception of the natural world resulted in two must-have books for school libraries and education-minded families, *The Golden Book of Biology* (1961) and *The Animal Kingdom* (1968).

Harper illustrated birds and other subjects in a distinctive style at odds with the naturalistic style of conventional bird painters. He called it "minimal realism." As he often said, "I don't count the feathers on the wings, I just count the wings."

Harper produced earlier paintings using gouache and, later, acrylic paints, but his principal print medium was serigraphy, an arduous process involving stencil cutting and sequential printing of as many as thirty-seven colors through a silkscreen press. He used blocks of color as geometric shapes to capture the essential characteristics of an animal. Cardinals, one of his favorite subjects, often resemble fighter planes in flight, while the bird in the print *House Wren on Clothesline*, is aptly domesticated with the addition of wood clothespins on

PRECEDING PAGES: A bird rendered in two dimensions, without nuances of light or shade, not to mention feathers, nevertheless acquires a striking dynamism— the cardinal as fighter plane—characteristic of Charley Harper's graphic genius. ABOVE: Harper's career took off in the 1950s after a number of his drawings appeared in *Ford Times,* a magazine published by the Detroit automaker to encourage interest in travel and travel-related activities such as bird watching. OPPOSITE: Fashion designer Todd Oldham, who has championed Harper's work, has collected a wide range of Charley's vintage 1950s silkscreen prints for his Pennsylvania country house. The furniture shown here is covered in fabric designed by Oldham in a style deliberately evoking the art of Charley Harper.

the laundry line on which it perches. Harper liked to joke that he was probably the only American wildlife artist never to have been compared to John James Audubon. Nicholas Hammond, an English wildlife art expert, recently did just that, claiming that both artists are masters of composition above all else.

The captions Harper typed out for his illustrations on a 1926 Royal manual typewriter are more like prose poems or haiku, in a style inspired by E. B. White, who originally provided the short texts for Charley's birds in *Ford Times*. In one issue, for example, White described the song of the whip-poor-will as "one of the sweetest in the orchestra of night," and identified the mourning dove as "a sweet, melancholy bird, mourning the passing of days, the transitoriness of life, the depletion of requited love."

In Harper's own work, the puns and alliterations come fast and furiously. Titles of his serigraphs and lithographs included *Coniferous Cardinal*, *Gregarious Grosbeaks*, *B-r-r-r-rdbath* (winter scene), *Ternscape*, and *Vowlentine*. He called the image of a feeding pileated woodpecker *Antypasto* in his first published book, *Birds & Words* (1974, reprinted 2009). For *Crow in Snow*, in his book *Beguiled by the Wild* (1994), he wrote: "Crows are black birds and blackbirds are also, but a crow in the snow is so much the more so."

A staunch environmentalist, Harper railed against the arrival of huge Caterpillar tractors on land being developed near him in Cincinnati. He called them, collectively, Backhoesaurus, and tartly observed that the project, called Quail Hollow Condos, was named after creatures that were destroyed to build it. Brett, who serves as director of Charley Harper Art Studio, recalls how passionate his father was on the subject. "We felt that statements, polemics of concern about global issues, were vital," he says. "Who can do this more powerfully than an artist?"

Harper executed posters for the National Park Service and for bird observatories at Cape May, New Jersey, and Hawk Mountain in Pennsylvania. Brett says his father did a lot of his work gratis if he thought the causes were worthy, including four large-scale tile murals in public buildings. The Cornell Laboratory of Ornithology invited him to Ithaca, New York, for the unveiling of his 2005 poster *We Think the World of Birds*, in which planet earth is portrayed as a bird's egg.

"I'm sitting in this room," Charley Harper said at the ceremony, "surrounded by Louis Agassiz Fuertes' paintings and filled with awe because he was one of the first artists who did birds so well." He then added, "Of course, I'd never do it that way myself."

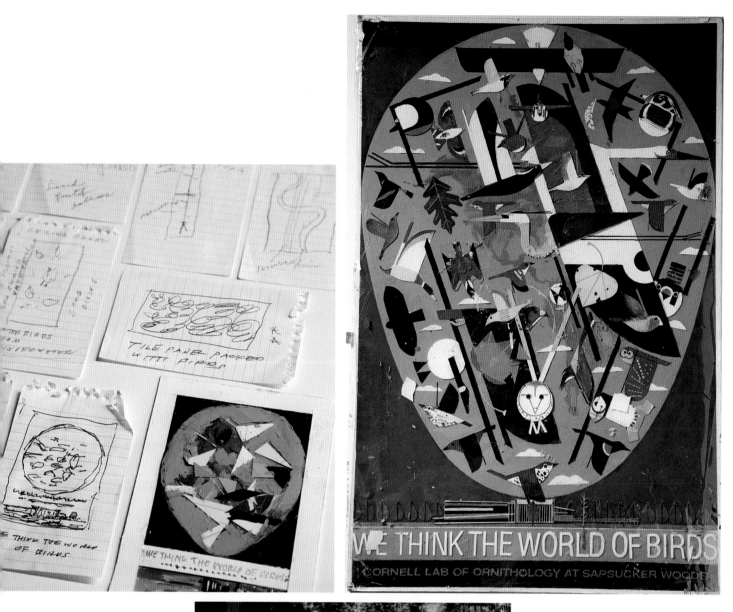

OPPOSITE AND ABOVE: Mock-ups showing Harper's artistic process reveal his meticulous regard for composition and line. The poster, *We Think the World of Birds,* created for the Cornell Lab of Ornithology, depicts an egg-shaped planet teeming with birds. LEFT: Brett Harper carries on the artistic tradition of his parents at the Charley Harper Studio in suburban Cincinnati, where a giant painted likeness of a ladybug greets visitors with the message that Harper's whimsical spirit lives on.

MARA AND THE SWAN

W HAT WAS PARADISE BUT A GARDEN," MUSES THE
BLUEBIRD ON ONE OF THE PORCELAIN "TALKING BIRD"
VASES BY MARA SUPERIOR. HER CERAMIC PIECES, WHICH BLEND
SOPHISTICATION AND WHIMSY, ARE REPRESENTED IN THE WHITE
HOUSE COLLECTION OF AMERICAN CRAFTS, THE SMITHSONIAN
AMERICAN ART MUSEUM, AND NUMEROUS OTHER MUSEUMS. BIRDS
ARE UBIQUITOUS IN HER WORK, OFTEN WITH WORD BALLOONS
OVER THEIR HEADS OFFERING COMMENTARY, QUOTATIONS, AND
OBSERVATIONS ON THE WORLD.

"I was raised in an era when animals were verbal creatures. Bambi, Dumbo,
Babar, and so many of the characters in fairy tales all talked," she says, "so I'm
inclined to give them something to say when their images appear in my own
cast of characters." That cast includes a swan, geese, herons, and the long lost
dodo, plus all the garden variety birds she observes through the windows of her
1828 Greek Revival home in western Massachusetts. The ducks featured in her
work are inspired by the mallards she sees on the pond near her studio. "Their
feathers and markings make a very graphic statement and they each have such
different personalities," observes Mara.

PRECEDING PAGES: Mara Superior's sculptural teapot, "A Swan's Wedding Day," was inspired by the artist's discovery that swans practice monogamy. ABOVE: The artist at home. ABOVE RIGHT: A "talking bird" vase is Mara's interpretation of a classical eighteenth-century vase form. The one bluebird depicted is saying, "What was paradise but a garden?" OPPOSITE: Mallard ducks are celebrated on the table centerpiece created by Mara. The framed watercolor hanging on the wall was done by Roy Superior as a tribute to a sparrow that had crashed into a window and died.

Mara often depicts farm animals, especially cows, pigs, and chickens. Growing up in New York in a large Italian family, she recalls that many of her relatives owned parakeets and parrots and that her grandmother miraculously produced five or six yellow chicks in the backyard on Easter Sunday every year, to the delight of Mara and her cousins.

Mara attended Manhattan's famed High School of Art and Design. Frequent visits to the Metropolitan Museum of Art, near which she lived, provided lasting influences on her own art. "I particularly loved the ibises in the Egyptian collection," she recalls, "but my favorite bird was the swan, with its graceful beauty and the fact that it mates for life." Renaissance paintings depicting the Greek myth of Leda and the Swan also made a strong impression on her, especially Leonardo da Vinci's version. The painting shows Zeus in the form of a swan pressing his attentions upon the unsuspecting and innocent Leda. William Butler Yeats wrote a superheated poem about the encounter, famously beginning "A sudden blow: the great wings beating still / Above the staggering girl . . ."

Five swans are depicted in a more benign form in Mara's piece *A Swan's Wedding Day*, an elaborate sculptural teapot that was featured in an exhibition at the Peabody Museum in Salem, Massachusetts. Inspirational images in Mara's studio include Audubon's iconic *Whistling Swan* print and a reproduction of Giotto's thirteenth-century painting *St. Francis Preaching to the Birds*.

For Mara, the discovery of porcelain and its magical glass and jewel-like qualities had a transformative effect on her career as an artist. Approaching

each of her pieces as if she were making a sculpted canvas, Mara works with brilliant white English china clay and three oxide colors—copper for red, cobalt for blue, and chrome for green—as well as many underglazes that work at the highest temperatures reached in her gas-fired kiln.

A number of Mara's works are on display throughout her house, often in or on handmade furniture created by her husband, painter and sculptor Roy Superior. The couple have collaborated on a series of cabinets, several of which have found their way into museums. Roy is as bird-centric as Mara. As a graduate student in painting at Yale, he took an elective course in ornithology and has remained an ardent birder ever since. Many of his early watercolors were images of birds. A dedicated fly fisherman, Roy usually carries binoculars out on the stream.

"An observant angler can tell when certain insects that trout feed upon are hatching because the birds go into a feeding frenzy over the river," he says. "I've seen a bird actually pick my floating dry fly off the water, fortunately dropping the imitation before getting too far. It would have been difficult to land a swooping swallow."

OPPOSITE: Behind the Lacanche gas stove from France are decorative tiles, handmade and hand-painted by the lady of the house, and depicting birds, butterflies, and flowers. The window niche was created to provide a glimpse of the natural world. ABOVE: Mara and Roy's refrigerator serves as a kind of bulletin board containing images for consideration by the couple for future artistic projects.

ONE MAN'S PECKING ORDER

IMAGINE YOU'VE JUST HAD A BABY GIRL AND A FRIEND BRINGS YOU A MOBILE HE HAS CONSTRUCTED TO HANG OVER HER CRIB. THE MOBILE IS MADE OF TINY BIRDS FASHIONED FROM THE TIN OF A MEDAGLIA D'ORO COFFEE CAN AND SUSPENDED FROM A HORSESHOE-SHAPED WIRE. MORE TO THE POINT, THE MOBILE MAKER IS ALEXANDER CALDER. NO WONDER THAT WHEN DAUGHTER ELISE GETS AROUND TO UTTERING HER FIRST WORD, IT'S "BIRDS."

Artist and antiques dealer John Sideli worked for "Sandy" Calder and his wife, Louisa, for two years as a young man, overseeing the artist's estate in Roxbury, Connecticut, in exchange for free lodgings and studio space. Early in his tenure, John and his then wife, Jackie, were invited to a cocktail party at the Calders' so that they could get to know the neighbors.

"William Styron was there," recalls John. "Mike Nichols was there. Arthur Miller was there. We were a little . . . intimidated."

Following his stint with the Calders, John hit the road as a "picker," a job colorfully portrayed in the Larry McMurtry novel *Cadillac Jack*. Instead of a Cadillac, John used a van to make the rounds of antiques shops, flea markets, and tag sales in search of art and articles of bonafide quality, interest—and resale value. His eye for the unusual and instinct for the potential in found objects culminated in his first venture into real estate.

PRECEDING PAGES: Atop the
Victorian diorama are two pieces
illustrating John Sideli's "feel for unusual
and distinctive elements with graphic
line," as one London folk art dealer has
stated, including *Rare Bird* with its long
legs and turkey-feather tail. ABOVE:
John Sideli at home in Wiscasset, Maine.
ABOVE RIGHT: Eggs collected from a
game farm are given visual appeal with
the addition of a Victorian glass dome.
OPPOSITE: John's living room displays
several of his creations, including an
acrylic kestrel painted in the 1970s and
a stylized take on penquins entitled
Harlequins.

John literally moved into a houseful of antiques, buying an 1820 violin maker's house in the village of Malden Bridge in Columbia County, New York. The house went for $20,000, but the real bargain was the $1,500 he paid for its contents. He lived in Malden Bridge for twenty-seven years. When he wasn't buying and selling antiques, he painted and cobbled together objects he found in his travels to create pieces of folk art, sometimes in the image of birds.

"I often like to begin with a title and work backward from there, looking for pieces that can express my idea," he explains. His idea for *Rare Bird*, for example, resulted in his combining narrow sticks of wood to create the impression of a long-legged wading bird, then adding a turkey feather for its tail. "At other times," he says, "I will simply juggle the selected elements until they speak to me, to tell a story or define a concept." He made a home for a stuffed Canada goose with a discarded glass case, strewing seashells on the floor of it to suggest a Victorian cabinet of curiosities. There are also times when John knows things are better left as is, such as the pair of carved duck heads he came upon and still has on display in his living room. "Sometimes fragments of things can speak volumes more than the totality," he observes, "and do so with more grace."

John says his interest in nature began with a fascination for snakes as a child. For a time he collected them, feeding them with lab mice that he kept in the family's freezer, against his mother's better judgment. Years later, when his brother Vincent Sideli (see page 59) and Vincent's wife, Carol, took up birding as young schoolteachers, John often tagged along. His most memorable encounters with birds occurred when he lived on Costa Rica's Nicoya Peninsula for three years.

"To go birding in Costa Rica, all you had to do was look out your front window." John observes, "There were mango and banana trees in the yard, and they attracted all kinds of birds. We'd put out bunches of overripe bananas and watch as six or eight toucans fed upon them. I'd see the migrating birds from New England down there in the winter. It was not uncommon for five or six male orioles to perch next to each other on a single branch, a sight you'd never enjoy in breeding season up north."

After his Caribbean stay, he moved to Wiscasset, Maine, and opened his own antiques shop. The art of the deal in antiquing circles is often based on word of mouth among trusting friends. Not long ago John got a call from a friend in Binghamton, New York, who told him, "Something rather extraordinary walked into my house today." The something was a group of carved birds found in an attic, and the birds looked old. John drove to Binghamton to investigate.

John relates his visit. "My friend sat me down in a wing chair in his living room. His wife brought the birds in one at a time. Pretty soon I had an armful of them, like kittens. There were ten birds in all, five yellowlegs and five plovers. From the way they were painted, I suspected they dated from the 1880s." Later, John received confirmation from a specialist in the field of bird carvings that the birds did indeed rank high in the pecking order of such antiques. "The yellowlegs were especially beautiful." John recalls, "each one was carved in a different posture. I was so nervous, and at the same time so excited, that I was shaking."

His friend asked John if he wanted to make an offer. John wondered if his friend could at least give him a price range. The friend demurred. John finally came up with a number, all he could afford at the time, and one that he thought was probably too low to close the deal.

"Let me make a call," his friend said, and left the room. Minutes later he returned. "They're yours," he declared.

Weeks later, John sold the birds to a collector in Maine for a handsome profit, and they are still in that man's hands some years later.

OPPOSITE: A nineteenth-century print of an eagle drawn with a patriotic motif soars over a folk art bird and a Victorian classroom tool for teaching the alphabet. ABOVE: A theorem painting and a bird on a compote of fruit hangs on one wall.

TOP AND ABOVE LEFT: The eagle is a favorite motif, whether on an antique fireman's helmet or a stately gilded weathervane. ABOVE RIGHT: John Sideli's own version of a Victorian cabinet of curiosities. OPPOSITE: Combining disparate elements is one way Sideli makes an artistic statement. He arranged the Canada goose on a surface of seashells inside the Victorian glass cabinet.

DIGGING FOR ANTIQUES

Birds and gardens go together, so when a botanical garden serves as a venue for an antiques show, as often happens, there is a strong likelihood that birdy things will be found among the offerings on tables and under tents. Looking for those special finds is a great way to spend a summer weekend. The Antiques in the Garden show, sponsored by the Coastal Maine Botanical Gardens and the Maine Antiques Dealers Association, is one such annual affair.

Like flea markets, antiques shows are unpredictable resources for collectors looking to add something with the patina of age and distinction to their homes. Yet they are always entertaining. One may go home empty-handed but not dispirited. Like the bird arriving at a feeder after the squirrels have come through, the garden show antiquer simply shrugs off the frustration and flies off to the next target on the list.

FEATHERING THE NEST: DECORATING WITH AN AVIAN THEME

YOU CAN TRACE OUR FASCINATION WITH BIRDS THROUGH-OUT THE HISTORY OF ART," SAYS KATHY KELSEY FOLEY, DIRECTOR OF THE LEIGH YAWKEY WOODSON ART MUSEUM IN WAUSAU, WISCONSIN, WHICH HAS ORGANIZED AN ANNUAL BIRDS IN ART EXHIBIT FOR SEVERAL DECADES. PART OF THE APPEAL OF BIRDS TO EARTHBOUND HUMANS IS THEIR ABILITY TO FLY. "BUT ARTISTS ALSO CAN'T RESIST THE EXOTIC NATURE AND ENVIRONMENTS OF BIRDS," OBSERVES FOLEY. "AND MANY TEXTILE DESIGNERS, CLOTHING DESIGNERS, AND INTERIOR DESIGNERS DRAW THEIR MOTIFS FROM A VAST REFERENCE BANK OF VISUAL MATERIALS ON BIRDS, WHETHER THEY ARE CHINESE PORCELAINS, DUTCH PAINTINGS, JAPANESE SILKS OR SCROLLS, OR EVEN MEDIEVAL MANUSCRIPTS FEATURING SOME OF THE MOST EXQUISITE IMAGES OF BIRDS IN PRINT."

Bird lovers today have no shortage of avian images to incorporate in their home décor, if they so desire, and no shortage of decorators and designers who are conversant with the wide range of materials available to dress out a living room, a bedroom, a study or den, or an entire house with elegance and originality. Moreover, these creative forces in home fashions and the allied arts understand the larger context in which birding themes play a role.

PRECEDING PAGES: In a traditional living room, the "Hootie" owl print fabric adds a fun factor with a nod to the 1960s. Crows make their watchful presence felt on a pair of oil-on-board paintings by Michael Rousseau. ABOVE: A mantel swings, metaphorically, with the musical verve of Charlie "Bird" Parker. From left to right: a square platter with roadrunner by ceramic artist Hannah Niswonger; framed canary-in-a-cage wallpaper by York Wallcoverings; flight patterns from "Bird Series" by Mona Mark. On the shelves, bottles cast from old forms bear hand-drawn transfers of birds, nests, and eggs by Laura Zindel. The wood-fired stoneware vessel with abstracted avian form is by potter Sam Taylor. OPPOSITE: Birds figure prominently in the art of decoupage, a fashionable leisure activity in the 18th century. Decorative artist John Derian revives the art using reprints of hand-colored eighteenth- and nineteenth-century images that are cut and pasted onto glass.

ABOVE: "Bird wallpapers are so popular because they can be interpreted in many ways and therefore can seem personal to each individual," says Cindy Weil, owner of Wallpaper Collective. Left to right: "Nevermore" by Palace Papers through Wallpaper Collective incorporates swooping birds in a pattern reminiscent of traditional damasks; iconic peacock by Shand Kydd; ornithological print by Seabrook; Victorian-inspired birds, including tropical species, by York Wallcoverings.
OPPOSITE: Wallpapers and textiles with designs from abstract to ornithological capture bird life with style as in these examples of pillows and wall fabric from Thomas Paul.

Cindy Weil's company, the Wallpaper Collective, specializes in hand-screened designs on custom-colored papers, many of them featuring birds. "During the Gothic and Renaissance periods, before literacy was widespread, birds were part of a rich visual symbolism," she points out. "They were and still are shown in works of art not only as natural history but as symbols, storytelling figures, and surrogates for some facet of human experience.

"While commonplace in our own backyards," Cindy adds, "they remain wild and unpossessed by humans. Their ability to fly and their varied songs lend an air of mystery that sets them apart from other animals and makes them, quite frankly, irresistible."

Product designer Thomas Paul takes classic design motifs found in nature and presents them in stylized form on everything from fabrics to rugs to plates. "I use birds so often in my work because they are so appealing to a lot of people," he says. "Bird images work well with florals and plants and trees, and there's a long history of bird motifs in textile design." The range of imagery is inexhaustible—Chinese paper-cut birds, silhouetted perching birds, birds from antique engravings, calligraphic birds, parrots, nests, eggs, and birds in cages—and Paul still hasn't scratched the surface. "Every season I say, 'Okay, we're through with birds,' but inevitably I find some bird image I can't resist."

Vermont artist Laura Zindel combines her passion for ceramics and naturalistic illustrations of birds, nests, eggs, and insects to embellish her designs for tableware and other objects with surface patterns that call to mind the contents of a specimen case. "I'm drawn to those Victorian cabinets filled with treasures of art and wonders of the natural world," she says. "They touch something unexplainable and primal in me."

ABOVE: Artist Susan Mikula printed Polaroid photographs on ten-inch melamine plates to capture the now-you-see-them, now-you-don't quality of birds. ABOVE RIGHT: "The Owlcat" is a textile painting by Erica-Lynn Huberty, using traditional stitching along with small brush work on fabric. OPPOSITE: A plain wall benefits from the graphic appeal of bird silhouettes. The acrylic-on-paper painting and porcelain ceramics are by artist Mary Anne Davis. Displayed on cupboard shelves are a set of graduated porcelain bowls by Middle Kingdom.

In her textile paintings of birds, Erica-Lynn Huberty is more like a modern seventeenth-century naturalist, applying small brushwork and embroidery or other handwork to create a new iconography. "Birds have always held great symbolic meaning for me—freedom, flight, delicacy," she says. "The structure of a bird—its bones, shape, colors, feathers—is fascinating and wonderful to interpret. But I also admire the resilience of birds, and the fact that they are so tenacious in their survival skills."

The explosion of interest in bird watching is part of a larger devotion to conservation and the natural world. "I love the fact that birds have survived millions of years and that Darwin singled out finches to describe the theory of evolution," says Mary Anne Davis. Davis incorporates the likenesses of birds who come to her feeders in Chatham, New York, into contemporary ceramics and paintings. "I think we all need to pay more attention to birds and how they live, so that we might learn more sustainable ways of living ourselves."

Just as the Arts and Crafts Movement flourished from 1880 to 1910 in response to the dehumanizing effects of the Industrial Revolution, an emerging twenty-first-century design movement is reacting to crises affecting our climate and the environment and to reports of the degradation and disappearance of our natural habitats. Many artists and designers recognize that birds bring us back to nature and offer a sense of style and serenity in chaotic times.

ABOVE: For armchair birdwatchers, larger-than life studies of the nightingale, tyrant flycatcher, and thrush make a soft landing on the decorative linen pillows from Ox Bow Décor.

OPPOSITE: Quilt dealer Laura Fisher observes that birds were seldom used in traditional quilting but the needlework parrots on this vintage quilt are a showstopper. The stoneware jug by Michael Kline is decorated with hand-painted birds. An antique double-turret birdcage is appreciated for its architectural form.

"Birds come loaded with metaphor and meaning," says Leslie Ferrin of the Ferrin Gallery in Pittsfield, Massachusetts. "When the twin towers fell, I couldn't help but think of the canary in the mine. The artist is the canary, or messenger. Birds became symbolic by accident," she says, "and they were everywhere in art after that."

Birds are present in many forms throughout our culture. We study them for the things they tell us about their health and about the health of the environment. We admire them for their beauty, courage, and amazing behaviors. And they make us smile.

In spite of all the challenges in the world, both human created and natural, many bird people still retain their sense of humor, as the revival of interest in the work of Charley Harper, for example, would suggest. "We've gotten away from just literal interpretations of birds," notes collector Kathryn Precourt. "We want to feel close to nature, but we don't mind it if some of our birds are stylized and contemporary. Fun and funny are always welcome."

ROCK, PAPER, SCISSORS—AND BIRDS

Erika Soule never met a bird she did not like. "I grew up on a farm on an island in Maine," she says. "The outdoors was like my personal bird lab. There's this picture of me as a toddler with my thumb in my mouth and a live chicken tucked under my arm."

Erika's grandmother, a lifelong member of the Audubon Society, was a huge influence. "She was always calling us to report on the birds she had just seen in her yard," says Erika. "She believed we should all know the names of all the things around us, especially the flowers and birds. She instilled that belief in my mother, and my mother passed it along to me."

Erika's list of favorite birds includes the chickadee, "the state bird of Maine and probably the first one I was able to identify by sight and by sound," and the bowerbird, which she first read about as a child in one of her Golden nature books. "I was totally enthralled by the male's ritual of building this elaborate, three-foot-high spire of sticks and twigs on a platform of moss and decorated

with collections of nuts and beetles," she says, "all to attract a mate."

It came as no surprise that when Erika decided to open her shop—Rock Paper Scissors—in Wiscasset, Maine, birds and her interest in their habits and habitats would play a big role in defining her inventory. She has stocked the store just as a bowerbird might if it

went into retail. There is a wide variety of fanciful note cards sure to set customers tweeting to their birder friends. There are paintings from the seriously unpredictable imagination of artist Matt Adrian, with seriously inscrutable titles like *In this Poignant Moment of Finality, the Vibration of Atoms Sounds Like Singing.* Carved bird

calls come in colorful boxes resembling children's blocks. "The calls are made by a craftsman in France," says Erika, "and sometimes it takes him years to get the bird's song just right."

And that, said the robin to the worm, only scratches the surface.

BIRDING RESOURCES

CONSERVATION ORGANIZATIONS

American Bird Conservancy
4249 Loudon Avenue
P.O. Box 249
The Plains, VA 20198
(888) 247-3624
www.abcbirds.org

Mission: *To conserve native birds and their habitats throughout the Americas.*

American Birding Association
4945 North 30th Street
Suite 200
Colorado Springs, CO 80919
(800) 850-2473
www.aba.org

Mission: *To represent the North American birding community and support birders through publications, conferences, workshops, tours, partnerships, and networks. Its Birders' Exchange program solicits new and used birding equipment, field guides, and other educational materials for distribution to local scientists, conservationists, and educators in Latin America and the Caribbean.*

Publications: Birding, *a bimonthly;* Winging It, *a newsletter for members;* North American Birds, *a subscription quarterly reporting on seasonal and changing North American birdlife; and* A Bird's-Eye View, *a youth newsletter for students.*

National Audubon Society
225 Varick Street
New York, NY 10014
(212) 979-3000
www. audubon.org

Mission: *Through its members, state offices, and a network of some five hundred local chapters, nature preserves, and sanctuaries, Audubon pursues its mission to conserve and restore natural ecosystems, focusing on birds, other wildlife, and their habitats, for the benefit of humanity and the earth's biological diversity. Sponsor of the annual Christmas Bird Count, nationwide census of American bird populations.*

Bimonthly publication: Audubon *magazine*

National Wildlife Federation
11100 Wildlife Center Drive
Reston, VA 20190
(800) 822-9919
www.nwf.org

Mission: *To inspire Americans to protect wildlife for our children's future.*

Bimonthly publication: National Wildlife *magazine. Also, for young readers,* Ranger Rick *and* Wild Animal Baby.

The Nature Conservancy
4245 North Fairfax Drive
Suite 100
Arlington, VA 22203
(800) 628-6860
www.nature.org

Mission: *To preserve the plants, animals, and natural communities that represent the diversity of life on earth by protecting the lands and waters they need to survive.*

Quarterly publication: Nature Conservancy *magazine*

PUBLICATIONS

Bird Watcher's Digest
P.O. Box 110
Marietta, OH 45750
(800) 879-2473
www.birdwatchersdigest.com

Mission: *Bimonthly founded in 1976 by Elsa and Bill Thompson and still in family hands. Also available, a series of fifteen "backyard booklets" with useful information for birders on a variety of subjects.*

Related blogs: *billofthebirds.blogspot.com; juliezickefoose.blogspot.com*

Birder's World
Kalmbach Publishing Company
21027 Crossroads Circle
P.O. Box 1612
Waukesha, WI 53187
(800) 533-6644
www.BirdersWorld.com

Bimonthly for backyard bird watchers and serious birders alike.

SANCTUARIES AND NATURE CENTERS

John James Audubon Center at Mill Grove
1201 Pawlings Road
Audubon, PA 19403
(610) 630-2209, ext. 101
http://pa.audubon.org/centers_mill_grove.html

Audubon's first home in America (near Philadelphia) now serves as educational center, with a collection of art and taxidermy, on 175-acre estate of rolling woodlands and open meadows, a haven for birds and wildlife.

Black Swamp Bird Observatory
13551 West State Route 2
Oak Harbor, OH 43449
(419) 898-4070
www.bsbobird.org
www.biggestweekinamericanbirding.com

Research station and educational center located amid marshes and woodlands bordering Lake Erie in northwest Ohio, including Magee Marsh Wildlife Area. Sponsors bird festival, "The Biggest Week in American Birding," every spring.

Related blog: *Birdingwithkennandkim. blogspot.com*

Cape May Bird Observatory
Northwood Center
701 East Lake Drive
P.O. Box 3
Cape May Point, NJ 08212
(609) 884-2736
www.birdcapemay.org

With the New Jersey Aubudon Society, sponsors annual spring and fall bird festivals, with hawks, warblers, shorebirds, eagles, and owls the main attractions for birders.

Central Park
New York, NY
(718) 828-8262
rdcny@earthlink.net
www.birdingbob.com

Half-day bird walks led by evolutionary biologist Robert DeCandido and photographer Deborah Allen introduce visitors to hundreds of birds that make their home or pass through the park's abundant green space every year.

Gulf Coast Bird Observatory
103 West Highway 332
Lake Jackson, TX 77566
(979) 480-0999
www.gcbo.org

In partnership with other conservationist groups, works for solutions to ecological challenges in and around the Gulf of Mexico.

Hawk Mountain Sanctuary
1700 Hawk Mountain Road
Kempton, PA 19529
(610) 756-6961
www.hawkmountain.org

Historic refuge for birds of prey along eight miles of ridge and valley trails on 2,600 acres in southeastern Pennsylvania.

High Island Bird Sanctuaries
c/o Houston Audubon Society
440 Wilchester Boulevard
Houston, TX 77079
(713) 932-1639
www.houstonaudubon.org

Four self-contained nature preserves near Galveston, Texas.

Hog Island Audubon Camp
 c/o Project Puffin
159 Sapsucker Woods Road
Ithaca, NY 14850
(607) 257-6231
www.projectpuffin.org

Audubon's first nature center, founded in 1936, is located on a 330-acre island in Muscongus Bay near Damariscotta in midcoast Maine and hosts summer sessions of ornithological programs for beginning and experienced birders and teachers.

FESTIVALS

Potholes and Prairie Birding Festival
c/o Birding Drives Dakota
P.O. Box 26
Jamestown, ND 58401
(888) 921-2473
www.birdingdrives.com

Popular bird watching spectacle held in early June every year.

Space Coast Birding and Wildlife Festival
P.O. Box 517
Titusville, GA 32781
(800) 460-2664
www.spacecoastbirdandwildlifefestival.org

Prime stopover habitat for many fall-migrating shorebirds, waterfowl, raptors, and passerines (perching birds).

World Birding Center
WBC HQ at Bentsen–Rio Grande Valley State Park
2600 South Bentsen Palm Drive
Mission, TX 78572
(956) 584-9156
www.worldbirdingcenter.org

Network of nine birding sites along 120 miles of historic roads from scenic bluffs and wetlands to South Padre Island.

AVIAN SCIENCE

American Museum of Natural History
Central Park West at 79th Street
New York, NY 10024
(212) 769-5100
www.amnh.org

One of the world's preeminent scientific and cultural institutions, founded in 1869.

Burke Museum of Natural History and Culture
17th Avenue NE/NE 45th Street
Box 353010, University of Washington
Seattle, WA 98195
(206) 543-5590
www.washington.edu/burkemuseum/
collections/ornithology

With most of the museum's ornithology collection built in the past twenty years, emphasis is on the birds of Pacific Northwest, spread wings (largest in world with 26,000), and avian tissues.

Cornell Lab of Ornithology
159 Sapsucker Woods Road
Ithaca, NY 14850
(800) 843-2473
www.birds.cornell.edu

Mission: *To interpret and conserve the earth's biological diversity through research, education, and citizen science focused on birds.*

The Lab offers several programs of interest to bird watchers. In partnership with Audubon, eBird is a free online checklist program enabling birders to record their sightings online, among other services. Project FeederWatch is a fee-based program that encourages birders to report bird sightings at their own feeding stations on a regular basis, as part of a nationwide census effort. Birds of North America Online is an Internet-based field guide to the birds of North America, also available for a fee. With Audubon, the Lab also sponsors the Great Backyard Bird Count, an annual four-day event, usually staged in late February, with goals similar to the Audubon Christmas Bird Count.

www.ebird.org
www.birds.cornell.edu/pfw
bna-sales@cornell.edu
www.birdsource.org/gbbc

Quarterly publication: Living Bird, *features articles on bird biology and behavior, conservation, travel, and birding equipment.*

Florida Museum of Natural History
University of Florida Cultural Plaza
SW 34th Street and Hull Road
P.O. Box 112710
Gainesville, FL 32611
(352) 846-2000
www.flmnh.ufl.edu

The museum's ornithology program curates the world's fifth-largest collection of modern bird skeletons and the second-largest collection of bird sounds in the western hemisphere in the number of species.

Natural History Museum of Los Angeles County
900 Exposition Boulevard
Los Angeles, CA 90007
(213) 763-3466
www.nhm.org

Largest museum in the western United States with nearly 35 million specimens, including over 600 taxidermy mounts on exhibit in the Hall of Birds.

Smithsonian Institution

World's largest museum complex and research organization, composed of nineteen museums, nine research centers, and the National Zoo, including:

Smithsonian Migratory Bird Center
Smithsonian National Zoological Park
3001 Connecticut Avenue NW
Washington, DC 20008
P.O. Box 37012 MRC 5503
Washington, DC 20013
(202) 633-4240
www.nationalzoo.si.edu.scbi/
MigratoryBirds

Fosters greater understanding, appreciation, and protection of the phenomenon of bird migration.

Smithsonian National Museum of Natural History
10th Street and Constitution Avenue NW
Washington, DC 20560
(202) 633-1000
www.mnh.si.edu

Houses third-largest bird collection in world, with over 640,000 specimens representing about 80 percent of the approximately 9,600 known species of avifauna in the world.

Yale University Peabody Museum of Natural History
170 Whitney Avenue
New Haven, CT 06511
(203) 432-5050 (info tape)
www.peabody.yale.edu

AVIAN ART, CARVINGS, AND COLLECTIONS

Mass Audubon Visual Arts Center
963 Washington Street
Canton, MA 02021
(781) 821-8853
www.massaudubon.org/visualarts

Small museum on 140-acre nature preserve with several hundred miniature bird carvings and artwork by Audubon, Benson, Fuertes, and others.

New York Historical Society
170 Central Park West at 77th Street
New York, NY 10024
(212) 873-3400
www.nyhistory.org

Collection of 60,000 objects and works of art, including Hudson River School landscapes, masterpieces of colonial portraiture, and all 435 of Audubon's preparatory watercolors for Birds of America *(sold to the museum in 1863 by Audubon's widow). The watercolors are on limited exhibit of 40 per year to deter fading of color.*

Peacock Room
Freer and Sackler Galleries (Smithsonian)
Jefferson Drive at 12th Street SW
P.O. Box 37012, MRC 707
Washington DC 20013
(202) 633-1000
www.asia.si.edu

Once the dining room in the London home of a shipping magnate, this room was radically redecorated in a peacock motif in 1876–77 by the American-born artist James McNeil Whistler, then purchased by an American collector and moved to Detroit in 1904, and, later, in 1923, moved to its present location, where it remains on permanent display.

Roger Tory Peterson Institute of Natural History
311 Curtis Street
Jamestown, NY 14701
(800) 758-6841
www.rtpi.org

This compound of library, art collection, and nature center seeks to continue the legacy of Roger Tory Peterson (a native of Jamestown) by promoting the teaching and study of nature, to create knowledge of and appreciation and responsibility for the natural world. Sponsors annual birding festival and numerous educational events and art exhibitions.

Leigh Yawkey Woodson Art Museum
700 North 12th Street
Wausau, WI 54403
(715) 845-7103
www.lywam.org

Since 1976, the museum has hosted Birds in Art, *an annual juried exhibition seeking to present the best contemporary artistic interpretations of birds and related subject matter. The exhibition opens to the public on the first Saturday following Labor Day every year and is on view for nine weeks. The museum's permanent collection includes works by Audubon, N.C. Wyeth, Jasper Francis Cropsey, Albert Bierstadt, and Robert Bateman, and a sculpture garden with striking bird figures.*

ARTISTS, AUCTION HOUSES, ANTIQUES

Cherry Gallery
27 Church Street
Damariscotta, ME 04543
(207) 563-5639
www.cherrygallery.com

Specialists in quality rustic antiques often with bird motifs.

Copley Fine Art Auctions
Stephen O'Brien Jr.
268 Newbury Street
Boston, MA 02116
(617) 536-0030
www.copleyart.com

American sporting art auction company specializing in antique decoys and nineteenth- and twentieth-century American, sporting, and wildlife paintings. The Annual summer sporting sale (check website for dates) is a must for collectors of decoys, fishing collectibles, and related folk art.

Dennis and Dad Antiques
33 NH Route 119 East
Fitzwilliam, NH 03447
(603) 585-9479
www.dennisanddadantiques.com

Dealers in eighteenth- and nineteenth-century English ceramics, many of which feature bird designs. By appointment only.

Ferrin Gallery
437 North Street
Pittsfield, MA 01201
(413) 442-1622
www.ferringallery.com

One of the country's premier ceramic art and sculpture galleries, with changing exhibitions ranging from contemporary art, photography, and sculpture from throughout New England along with nationally known ceramic sculptors and studio potters. Artists represented by the gallery and featured in this book: Laura Zindel, Susan Mikula, Sam Taylor, Michael Kline, Michael Rousseau, Mary Anne Davis, Hannah Niswonger, Roy and Mara Superior, Middle Kingdom.

Laura Fisher's Fisher Heritage
305 East 61st Street
New York, NY 10065
(212) 838-2596
www.laurafisherquilts.com

Birds alight in this ever-changing inventory of antique quilts, hooked rugs, and American folk art.

Charley and Edie Harper Art Studio
699 Reynard Avenue
Cincinnati, OH 45231
(513) 522-0545
www.charleyharperartstudio.com

The Charley Harper Art Studio is dedicated to preserving and promoting the work of American illustrator Charley Harper. Online catalog of his work includes numerous avian images.

Erica-Lynn Huberty, artist
(631) 725-0927
www.ericalynnhuberty.com

Birds figure large in the fine art textile paintings by the artist available through:

The Silas Marder Gallery
120 Snake Hollow Road
Bridgehampton, NY 11932
(631) 702-2306
www.silasmarder.com

Sara Nightingale Gallery
21 North Ferry Road
Shelter Island, NY 11964
(631) 793-2256
sara@saranightingale.com
www.saranightingale.com

The Marston House
101 Main Street
Wiscasset, ME 04578
(207) 882-6010
www.marstonhouse.com

The storefront of Sharon and Paul Mrozinski offers a unique mix of eighteenth- and nineteenth-century textiles and furnishings with an emphasis on French. There is also a charming bed-and-breakfast on the property outfitted in beautiful essentials for a good night's rest.

Mona Mark, artist
(518) 766-3141
www.monamark.com

"Bird Series," an exploration of space and flight by the artist in black-and-white watercolor diptychs.

Moody Gallery
2815 Colquitt Street
Houston, TX 77098
(713) 526-9911
www.moodygallery.com

The gallery exhibits work by contemporary American artists with an emphasis on artists working and living in Texas as well as those with a strong connection to Texas. Artists represented by the gallery and in

some cases featured in this book: Luis Jimenez, James Drake, Bill Steffy, Ed Hill and Suzanne Bloom, Helen Altman, Jim Love, Al Souza, and Lisa Ludwig.

Kay O'Toole Antiques and Eccentricities
1921 Westheimer
Houston, TX 77098
www.kayotooleantiques.com

Carefully edited selection of mostly Swedish, Belgian, French, and Italian antiques and eccentricities such as French birdcages, spotted on a visit.

Peggy McClard Antiques: Americana & Folk Art
Houston, TX
(713) 880-2572
www.peggymcclard.com

Antiques dealer specializing in eighteenth- and nineteenth-century American folk art: painted birds, watercolors, Scherenschnitte, bird carvings, bird trees, flourishings. By appointment only.

Panteek
David and Sue Panken
P.O. Box 8208
Spokane, WA 99203
(888) 726-8335
www.panteek.com

Original antique bird prints of every description, including John Gould's nineteenth-century hummingbird collection; nests, eggs, and birds by Francis Orpen Morris, English, nineteenth century; seventeenth-century ornithological prints by English artist Francis Willoughby; and Audubon's Birds of America first-edition prints.

James Prosek, artist
Represented by Waqas Wajahat
P.O. Box 1100
New York, NY 10013
(212) 219-1817
www.waqaswajahat.com

Agent specializing in post-war and contemporary art, including the work of James Prosek, featured in this book and photographed with permission of artist and agent.

Salt Flats Photography
414 South Austin Street, #9
Rockport, TX 78382
(361) 288-2752
www.saltflatsphotography.com

Part art gallery, part backyard birding store. Owner and photographer Diane Loyd's love of Texas Gulf Coast birdlife is on view on one side of the store, the Rockport Gallery, and everything from seeds to feeders fills the other side, known as "4 the Birds."

John Sideli Art & Antiques
43 Middle Street
Wiscasset, ME 04578
(207) 882-6281
Open by chance or appointment
johnsideli@hotmail.com

Eclectic range of antiques and art including avian-themed prints, paintings, and original folk art by John Sideli.

BIRDS FOR THE GARDEN

Antiques and Garden Show of Nashville
P.O. Box 50950
Nashville, TN 37205
(605) 352-1282
www.antiquesandgardenshow.com

Every February, the "birds" return to this premier antiques and garden show: birdbaths, birdhouses, weathervanes.

Antiques in the Garden
Coastal Maine Botanical Gardens
www.mainegardens.org

This annual mid-July ritual celebrates gardens and American antiques. Spotted in the aisles: owl andirons, carved eagles, folk art puffins from the best of New England dealers.

Audubon Shop
907 Boston Post Road
Madison, CT 06443
(203) 245-9056
www.theaudubonshop.com

A must-visit stop for birders. Known as the place in Connecticut (and the country) for optical equipment, international travel and field guides, and expert advice from owners, Jerry and Janet Connolly.

Bird Cookies
35 Water Street
Richmond, ME 04357
(207) 737-2404

"Treats for the tweets" is how Mo Babicki describes the homemade bird cookies she makes from organic seed, berries, and flowers. Designs include sunflowers and hearts and seasonal varieties for holidays, winter, summer, and fall.

Birdhouses by Architectural Editions
Pinehurst, NC 28374
(910) 295-2717
www.architecturaleditions.com
rtbarch@nc.rr.com

"Upscale homes for sophisticated birds." This family business located in Pinehurst,North Carolina, specializes in designer birdhouses by architect Richard T. Banks, including miniature versions of Victorian high-style, Italianate, cottage, geometric, and whimsical designs.

Chicago Botanical Garden: Antique and Garden Fair
1000 Lake Cook Road
Glencoe, IL 60022
(847) 835-5440
www.chicago-botanic.org/antiques/

The best in classical and contemporary garden artifacts.

Nancy McCabe Garden Design
163 Dublin Road
Falls Village, CT 06031
(860) 930-8107
Ninanancy5000@hotmail.com

Garden designs emphasizing stonework, timber fencing, and native plants to create the unique and unusual, such as an Anglo-Indian-style garden and aviary.

Modern Bird Houses
(800) 496-7987
www.modernbirdhouses.com

For midcentury architecture buffs, modern classics for feathered friends handmade of harvested sustainable teak and based on actual case study designs by architects, including Richard Neutra.

Lynette Proler European Garden Ornaments
(310) 683-0868
www.garden-antiques.com

Fine European garden ornaments: birdbaths to aviaries.

Roderick Romero
Romero Studios
(646) 295-4325
www.romerostudios.com

Environmental artist and builder Roderick Romero designs one-of-a-kind treehouse "nests" to human scale. By commission only.

Terrain at Styer's
914 Baltimore Pike
Glen Mills, PA 19342
(610) 459-2400
www.shopterrain.com
http://shopterrain.com

Part of the Anthropologie family, this garden center and online store offers everything for the birder/gardener.

Jim Schatz, artist
(866) 344-5267
www.jschatz.com

Ceramic egg-shaped birdhouses and bird feeders in an array of glossy colors hand-crafted by the artist, available online and at many retail locations.

BIRDS FOR THE HOME

Acquire
61 Salem Street
Boston, MA 02113
(857) 362-7380
www.acquireboutique.com

Among the unusual and unique, new reproductions of eighteenth-century bird drawings.

Robert Allen
225 Foxboro Boulevard
Foxboro, MA 02035
(800) 333-3777
www.robertallendesign.com

Avian-themed fabric by Dwell Studio for Robert Allen, includes bird-patterned fabrics titled "Etched Aviary," "Vintage Blossom," and "Vintage Plumes."

Area
5600 Kirby Drive
Houston, TX 77005
(713) 668-1668

Interior designer Don Connelly's storefront is filled with European furniture old and new, twenty-first-century necessities, art, accessories, and tables piled high with books on interior design.

Bon
3022 E. Broadway
Tuscon, AZ 85716
(520) 795-2272
4419 North Campbell
Tuscon, AZ 85718
(520) 615-7690
www.bon-boutique.com

Avian art and accessories of many stripes: concrete birds for garden or house, bird bud vases, porcelain owls that light up, birds that perch on a wall, woven birdhouse nests, felt birds, and much more.

Calico Corners-Calico Home
(800) 213-6366
www.calicocorners.com

Bird-inspired fabric collections, available online and at retail locations listed on their website. Included is the Iman Collection, abstract avian designs by model turned textile designer Iman.

John Derian Company
6 East Second Street
New York, NY 10003
(212) 677-3917
www.johnderian.com

Decoupage artist John Derian, inspired by nineteenth-century engravings, decorates plates, plaques, platters, dishes, and more with nests, eggs, and birds.

Design Within Reach
903 Broadway
New York, NY 10010
(212) 477-1155
www.dwr.com

Bird in style: contemporary Italian birds sculptures, Eames house bird, Bertoia bird chair, and Audubon bird feeders are found at this retail shrine to modern design.

Duralee
www.duralee.com

Avian-themed textiles and wall coverings. To the trade only.

Etsy
www.etsy.com

An online artisan gallery and marketplace with over 150,000 entries just for bird-themed arts and crafts.

Evolution
120 Spring Street
New York, NY 10012
(212) 343-1114
www.theevolutionstore.com

Natural history collectibles: replicas of eggs, taxidermy, anatomical bird models.

Ox Bow Décor
99 Ox Bow Road
Weston, MA 02493
(781) 239-3546
www.oxbowdecor.com

Pillows and prints based on vintage botanicals and ornithological illustrations.

Thomas Paul
www.thomaspaul.com

Rugs, pillows, fabric, melamine tableware, many designed with a modern ornithological twist. Fabric: Through Duralee (www.duralee.com).

Pine Cone Hill Home Store
55 Pittsfield Road
Lenox, MA 01240
(413) 637-1996
www.pineconehill.com

Everything for feathering your nest with bedding, throw pillows, and table linens.

Rock Paper Scissors
68 Main Street
Wiscasset, ME 04578
(207) 882-9930

A home-focused boutique with an emphasis on design and birds, especially in art, including Charley Harper stationery and paintings by "Mincing Mockingbird" Matt Adrian.

F. Schumacher
79 Madison Avenue, 15th floor
New York, NY 10016
(800) 523-1200
www.fschumacher.com

"Modern Nature" wallpaper collection uses birds as a design motif in "Aviary," "A-Twitter," and "Birds and Butterflies." To the trade only.

Velocity Art and Design
251 Yale Avenue N.
Seattle, WA 98109
(206) 749-9575
www.velocityartanddesign.com

At Velocity Art and Design home furnishings and artwork embody standards of innovation, accessibility, humor, responsibility, visual joy—and birds: 139 bird design products pop up on a search of their website.

Wallpaper Collective
(917) 951-2081
www. wallpapercollective.com

The Wallpaper Collective specializes in small-run, screen-printed designs on high-quality paper by a select group of designers and artisans.

York Wallcoverings, manufacturer
750 Linden Avenue
York, PA 17404
(800) 375-9675
www.yorkwall.com

Bird-themed wallcovering collections.

ACKNOWLEDGMENTS

The authors thank the birding authorities and experts who helped us shape the scope and content of our work, most notably James Baggett, Jim Berry of the Roger Tory Peterson Institute, William Burt, Joseph Ellis, Kenn and Kimberly Kaufman, National Audubon Society ornithologist Stephen Kress, Audubon Medal–winning conservationist Donal O'Brien Jr., Stephen O'Brien, Dr. Noble Proctor, David Sibley, Bill Thompson III, Julie Zickefoose, and Dr. Kristof Zyskowski of New Haven's Peabody Museum.

Thanks to all the home owners who opened their doors to us and allowed us to photograph their bird-friendly habitats. They include Donna and Patrick Annunziata, Jan and Jack Cato, Don Connelly, Maria, Noah, and, especially, Alexander Gottdiener, Mary Jane and John Dreyer, Porter and Hollister Hovey, Judy and Robert Korostoff, Sharon and Paul Mrozinski, Adelaide Skoglund, and Carol and Vincent Sideli.

Artists whose works and workspaces grace our pages include Brett Harper, Lisa Ludwig, James Prosek, Roderick Romero, John Sideli, and Mara and Roy Superior. We thank them for their lively contributions.

Many galleries, shops, and collections added to our understanding of the beauty and impact of avian art. They include Ann and Dennis Berard, Leslie Ferrin, Laura Fisher, Betty Moody, and Erika Soule. In addition, the influential role of birds in decorating and design was brought home to us by Mary Anne Davis, Kathy Kelsey Foley, Todd Oldham, Tony Longoria, Erica-Lynn Huberty, Thomas Paul, Cindy Weil, and David and Sue Panken.

In city locales we received help and encouraging words from Kathy Baur, Fran and Dan Brennan, Carole Cusani, Nona Carmichael, Connie Chung and Maury Povich, Nikki Dalrymple, Annie Deguerin, Nancy Etheridge, Trish Foley, Joetta Moulden, Tessie Patterson, and Karen Terrell.

Friends in the country who aided and abetted us include Jill Connors, Kay Degenhardt, Chris Jerome, Cindy Lang, Laura Meyers, Julie Michaels, Ben Murray of Red Gate Farm, Bill Perlman, Geoffrey Precourt, and Lexi Walters Wright.

There were those who literally guided us through the natural wonders of the world of birds: Deborah Allen and Dr. Robert DeCandido in Central Park, Jean Bochnowski and Nancy Powell of the Audubon Center at Mill Grove in Pennsylvania, Ann Hoffert at the Potholes & Prairie Birding Festival of North Dakota, Nancy McCabe, the designer of extraordinary bird-friendly gardens, and Adam Wood at the High Island bird sanctuaries in Texas.

The creative team at Clarkson Potter brought out the best in us (we hope), especially our editor, Aliza Fogelson, production editor Terry Deal, editorial assistant Peggy Paul, production manager Joan Denman, art director Jane Treuhaft, and the book's inspired designer, Wayne Wolf. We also send a shout-out to an old friend, Lauren Shakely, for her early backing of the project.

Special thanks to Sara Stites for her help in organizing our immense photo log.

Finally, we thank our agents, Gayle Benderoff and Deborah Geltman, for all they have done for us past and present. With her personal passion for birds and birding, Gayle was the perfect goad and inspiration for us during the many months it took to piece together this particular nest. May it hold together! And if any eggs show up, they belong to her.

INDEX